PARACORD

FUSION TIES

VOLUME 2

Survival Ties, Pouches, Bars, Snake Knots, & Sinnets

D0869795

PARACORD FUSION TIES

VOLUME 2

Survival Ties, Pouches, Bars, Snake Knots, & Sinnets

Written & Photographed by
JD of *Tying It All Together*

4th Level Indie

Fusion Ties – Innovative ties created through the merging of different knot elements or knotting techniques.

Paracord Fusion Ties - Volume 2
by J.D. Lenzen
ISBN: 978-0-9855578-3-6

Published by *4th Level Indie*
Author's Site: fusionknots.com

Copyright ©2013 by J.D. Lenzen. All rights reserved.

No part of this book may be reproduced, stored in a retrieval system, or transmitted by any means, without written permission from the publisher, except by a reviewer, who may quote brief passages in a review where appropriate credit is given.

Because of the dynamic nature of the Internet, any web addresses or links contained in this book may have changed since publication and may no longer be valid. Further, any and all vendor information provided in this book does not constitute an endorsement or recommendation by the publisher or the author.

> **WARNING:** The bushcraft and tactical tying techniques (i.e., survival ties) described in this book are for use during circumstances where the safety of the individual is at risk. In turn, the publisher and author cannot accept any responsibility for any prosecutions or proceedings brought or instituted against any person or body as a result of the use or misuse of any technique described, or any loss, injury, or damage caused thereby.

Printed in the United States by BPR Book Group.

Distributed by Itasca Books Distribution.

Contents

Foreword

I've had a lifelong love of the outdoors, with a particular passion for the forests and mountains of the Northeastern U.S. I fondly recall trips to the woods with my father as a young boy in Massachusetts, walking beside him with a new pocketknife or bow and arrow set at my side. Between our walks and talks I'd make attempts to learn bow-drill and sun-lens fire starting methods with the tools we had on hand.

It was at this time in my life, about the age of 8, that I was introduced to knot tying by my grandfather, a World War II-era sailor with a knack for teaching. Many a day was spent by his side learning the Bowline, Monkey's Fist, and Round Turn and Two Half Hitches mooring tie. He also taught me macramé ties, including some better known today by manlier names, like the Cobra Stitch. I was a kid, spending time with my father and grandfather and having so much fun learning that I didn't realize I was gaining skills that would one day establish the foundation of my future bushcraft knowledge and knotting career.

Shortly after graduating from college with a degree in civil engineering I married, and my wife and I moved to New Hampshire to settle down and start a family. New Hampshire is the Live Free or Die state, and its White Mountains and 80% forest cover had called to me. And so it was, in the shadow of Mount Washington (near where I now live), that I committed myself to venture about on foot to see what natural wonders the region had to offer.

I'm a planner and a thinker by nature and a professional civil engineer by trade, so running headlong into the wilderness unprepared wasn't my style. As a result, before beginning my venture into the unknown I decided to first learn some basic skills, including traditional compass and map land navigation and firecraft. I built my own survival kit and gained knowledge of how to use its contents in the event of an emergency. I read books (and lots of them) written by those who'd already learned the techniques of wilderness survival, in many cases, the hard way. And I began participating in and learning from online forums related to bushcraft and survival.

It was during this period of my life, while I was reading about the importance of a basic survival kit, that I first considered working with paracord. A mantra of one of the books I was reading was to only carry gear that could serve multiple purposes. I figured that any gear made from paracord would do so in spades, because once unraveled the cordage served countless survival needs. So I acquired a skein of 550 paracord, dusted off an old knots and splices book my grandfather had given me, and set out to create some paracord works of my own.

One of the first things I did was improve upon the design of army ranger pace counter beads (used to tally steps in dead reckoning land navigation). Utilizing sliding Turks Head knots prevented breakage and unintentional movement common with the plastic beads on commercial sets. Soon I was making lanyards and handle grips for my hatchets

Foreword

and knives, zipper pulls that stored a ferro rod and tinder, sheaths, necklaces, and bracelet kits. My paracord creations could be characterized by the application of knots in innovative, utilitarian ways.

As the items I made started to gain notoriety in a handful of online forums, I began to create YouTube videos to teach others what I'd learned and discovered. While I'd inherited my grandfather's ability to teach, I soon found there was more to making a professional and effective video than hitting the record button and tying a knot.

Reviewing YouTube for insights into video production techniques, it is immediately apparent that all paracord-lined roads lead to J.D. Lenzen of *Tying It All Together* (TIAT). His videos are shot from the point of view of the tyer, with crystal clear focus and perfect lighting. His hands move fluidly through each step of his ties, never blocking his work, and always keeping perfect pace. Most impressively, he teaches the majority of his knots and ties to music, without uttering a single word.

Still, as much as J.D.'s production skills impress me, I'm more amazed by his wealth of original knotting designs. Week after week his videos present something interesting and new in an area I'd thought of as purely traditional. Unifying historical knots and weaves with innovative twists and turns of his own, J.D. produces fantastic results through a practice he refers to as fusion knotting.

Always the innovator, J.D.'s books expand upon his YouTube work, detailing his ties and techniques in a way his fusion knotting videos cannot. And with this book, *Paracord Fusion Ties - Volume 2* (PFT-V2), he pulls off another fusion of sorts—one of decorative and practical survival ties.

In the chapter titled Innovative Zipper Sinnets, J.D. drives a well deserved stake into the heart of the slow deploying Cobra Stitch bracelet. In Bushcraft and Tactical Ties, he offers ingenious paracord creations for unplanned hunt and gather and emergency situations. In Pouches, Baskets, & Secret Spaces he provides a variety of ways to store mini survival kits, or any other item you wish to carry or sock away. And every PFT-V2 lesson is presented in the same easy to follow, professional style that's made me a TIAT fan since the first time I saw the channel on YouTube.

Given my respect for J.D.'s videos and books, I'm honored to have been asked to write this foreword to PFT-V2. Presenting a massive breadth of decorative and practical tying insights, this book is a solid addition to the paracord fusion ties series, and a source of information you will no doubt enjoy.

Kevin G. Gagne (The Paracordist)
paracordist.com
May 2013

Acknowledgments

For their support and/or inspiration in the production of this book, I would like to thank Clifford W. Ashley, my parents (Jim and Barbara), Steve Davis, Laura Neil, Maynard Demmon and his kids (Cailean, Hailey, and Hayden), Josh Greenwalt, the subscribers to my *Tying It All Together* YouTube channel, and the members of the fusion knotting community as a whole. Without you, especially those who continue to support my online videos, this book would not have come to be.

And…

A very special thanks to my wife and muse, Kristen Kakos. Your presence in my life brings me joy, comfort, and the freedom to create. For these gifts I am forever grateful.

Introduction

Every knot ever tied exists within a single length of cord. Think about that for a moment. If you're holding a length of cord in your hand—which if you're reading this book you likely are (or soon will be)—you have in your possession the means for making a vast number of knots and ties. I consider this fact every time I pick up a length of cord. Its implications inspire me and establish the foundation upon which all my knots and ties are designed. This said, no other material I've found exemplifies a length of cord's potentiality better than paracord.

Whether you need to secure a load, build a shelter, make a bow drill, replace a broken shoelace, craft a primitive weapon, or improvise a belt for your pants, paracord can make it happen. Because of these and other uses for it, paracord tying communities have sprouted up all over the world. Unified by the Internet, some within these communities are motivated by the direct use of paracord, while others are drawn to the ties used to carry it around for later use. Whichever camp you find yourself in, this book, *Paracord Fusion Ties – Volume 2* (PFT-V2), covers both these bases and more.

Following this introduction, you'll find crisp, clear, full-color step-by-step instructions for bracelets, straps, and key fobs, as well as medallions and other storage ties that will keep your paracord on-hand and ready for deployment. Still PFT-V2 doesn't stop there. It also provides directions for ties and techniques that represent the next level in paracording knowledge—the making of practical paracord objects.

Primarily designed to provide survival and/or tactical advantages, practical paracord objects are in themselves useful. That is, they provide benefits to those who tie them, in real time; as opposed to when they're unraveled and the cord within them used. Examples of the practical paracord objects in PFT-V2 include the following:

- Bush Sandals - a reliable source of foot protection, allowing a person to jump, climb, and run while avoiding damage to the feet;

- Emergency Snow Goggles - a means of reducing eye exposure to UV light, and so preventing or mitigating snow blindness;

- No-Slip Machete Grip - a tie that decreases the chances of a machete being pulled from the hand while chopping or swinging; and

- Single-Cord Rock Sling - an improvised weapon that can be tied in minutes, allowing its user to protect themselves or effectively target prey.

The above are just a few examples of the many practical paracord objects featured in PFT-V2. There are many others waiting to be learned!

So whether you find yourself stranded in a desert, slogging through a temperate rain forest, pressing across icy tundra, or any other environment where paracord is on hand, the practical paracord objects in this book could one day save your life.

Introduction

Still, as stylish, useful, and/or potentially lifesaving the ties in PFT-V2 are, this book's purpose isn't solely to instruct. More so it's to construct, in your mind, a new way of thinking about paracord. As stated in the opening paragraph of this introduction, "Every knot ever tied exists within a single length of cord." This fact not only applies to the knots and ties described in this book. It applies to all knots and ties, past, present, and future.

Put another way, the instructions in PFT-V2 are merely examples of what can be achieved by fusion knotting—the creation of innovative knots and ties through the merging of different knot elements or knotting techniques.

Of course you could learn the 35 ties in PFT-V2 and nothing more, and greatly improve your skill set by doing so. But why stop there?

Once you feel comfortable with and clearly understand what is presented in this book, you could mix and match the component parts you learn. When you've created something you like, recognize, or find useful, set that piece aside, and mix and match some more. If you do this, and you're like me, you will soon have hundreds of new knots and ties of your own. Knots and ties you too can share with the world.

I'm often asked how I come up with the knots and ties I present in my various books and on my YouTube video channel, *Tying It All Together*. The short answer, I do exactly what I just proposed you do. I apply the principles and techniques of

fusion knotting, again and again. Only I do so every single day.

This, coupled with years of research, reading, and study have brought me to a point where knotting is now a language, a natural expression of my thoughts and ideas. Twists, turns, and loops have become like letters; knots and ties like words and sentences. Single cords make simple words and short sentences. And two or more cords make complex words and compound sentences. With this "language" I call fusion knotting, I write poetry and prose with cord. This may sound unconventional, but honestly, it's what I experience when I tie.

So learn what you can from PFT-V2, the other volumes in the paracord fusion ties series, or any other book beyond those. But remember, no book can ever come close to the original knots and ties you're capable of creating on your own.

In the words of Clifford W. Ashley (author of *The Ashley Book of Knots*), in a 1925 letter he sent to A.L. Sessions, editor of *Sea Stories Magazine*:

"I have invented a great many new practical and decorative knots and a new method of making sennit with any desired cross section shape, in fact several different methods and dozens of different shapes."

And just like Ashley, you too can build upon what's known, generate something new, and fill the world with pioneering knowledge. With this book, my hope is to assist you in that endeavor. In turn, the

Introduction

lessons you're about to learn aren't meant to demonstrate what I can do. They're meant to demonstrate what you can do. So read forward, reconfigure what's presented, and make something new!

JD of *Tying It All Together*

About Paracord

Background

Paracord is a lightweight nylon rope constructed with a core of yarns wrapped in a woven exterior sheath. The yarns of paracord establish the maximum stress the rope can withstand while being stretched or pulled, and the exterior sheath protects the yarns from abrasion. The word *paracord* derives from its original use as suspension lines for U.S. parachutes during World War II. This said, on account of paracord's utility, paratroopers used it for a variety of other tasks once on the ground.

As with other materials and technologies originally slated for military use, paracord has since become widely valued in civilian circles. Its commercial availability (not surprisingly) was initially pressed forward by military veterans who'd grown accustomed to its use during service. Over the years, support for its availability has been equally heralded by gun and knife collectors, hunters, survivalists, do-it-yourself (DIY) makers, as well as an ever-growing community of paracord crafters.

Types

The U.S. military describes six types of paracord (Type I, IA, II, IIA, III, and IV). However, for the purposes of the information provided in this book and the fundamental "need to know" knowledge of the readers, paracord is generally available in two forms, Type II and III. Type II paracord is conventionally called 450 paracord (minimum strength 450 pounds) and usually has a core consisting of 4 two-ply yarns. Type III paracord is referred to as 550 paracord (minimum strength 550 pounds) and typically has a core consisting of 7 two-ply yarns.

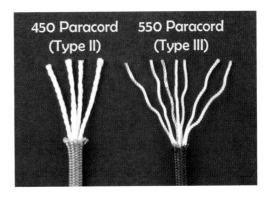

The ties presented in this book were created with 450 paracord. I used 450 paracord because I enjoy its pliability (it's very amenable to fusion knotting techniques) and the variety of colors it comes in. However, 550 paracord and a wide variety of other cord types, including (but not limited to) solid braid nylon, hemp, satin, fabric, leather cords, and even wire, could be used to create all the designs shown in this book. In short, when in doubt, give it a tie!

Sources

If you are living in the U.S., your paracord purchasing options are many, and include army surplus stores, hardware stores, and (in some communities) arts and craft stores. Be this as it may, not all people reading this book live in the U.S. or have access to (local) storefront paracord vendors. If this is you, don't worry. Thankfully, there are a growing number of worldwide paracord vendors, and most allow purchases online.

About Paracord

The following is a list of 45 online paracord vendors from a variety of domestic and international sources. My hope is that one of them will meet your paracord needs.

armynavystoreinc.com	paracord.com	stores.ebay.com/Five-Star-EDC
atlanco.com	paracord.no	stores.ebay.com/ParaClocks
atwoodrope.net	paracordcity.com	supplycaptain.com
bucklerunner.com	paracordplanet.com	survival-pax.com
campingsurvival.com	paracord-spain.es	takknife.com
cheaperthandirt.com	paracordstore.com	the550cordshop.com
coolglowstuff.com	redflarekits.com	thebushcraftstore.co.uk
countycomm.com	repmart.jp	theparacordstore.co.uk
delksarmynavysurplus.com	rothco.com	topbrassmilitary.com
extac.com.au	rwrope.com	touwhandel.nl
gorillaparacord.com	sankowebshop.jp	ubraidit.com
greatadventure.ca	sgtknots.com	uscav.com
myparacord.de	shoprobbys.com	vtarmynavy.com
onestopknifeshop.com	sosakonline.com	whitemoosetradingco.com
parachute-cord.com	stores.ebay.com/AnS-Tactical	wholesale-parachute-cord.com

Note: Because of the dynamic nature of the Internet, any web addresses or links contained in this book may have changed since publication and may no longer be valid. Further, any and all vendor information provided does not constitute an endorsement or recommendation by the publisher or the author.

About This Book

Instruction Format

The intent of this book is to provide all the information necessary to successfully complete each knot or tie presented while minimizing redundant procedures. For example, procedures performed on every knot or tie, such as snipping and singeing, are shown only once (see Page xxi) and then simply referenced as a procedure to be performed in the instruction text (i.e., "Carefully snip and singe the cord ends.").

In those cases when a finishing knot is routinely used, such as the 2-Strand Diamond Knot and the 4-Strand Diamond Knot, the instruction text calls out the knot to be tied accompanied by the page number where that knot was first shown. These "notable knots," as well as others, are detailed further in the next section.

Notable Knots

The following four knots are incorporated into multiple ties within this book:

- **2-Strand Diamond Knot** (Page 4)
- **Wall Knot (Collapsed)** (Page 43)
- **4-Strand Diamond Knot** (Page 50)
- **6-Strand Diamond Knot** (Page 58)

The 2-Strand Diamond Knot is used to assist in the clasping of bracelets. The 4-Strand Diamond Knot, the Wall Knot (Collapsed), and 6-Strand Diamond Knot are used to fix or lock a tie in place. Aside from allowing the clean finishing of a tie, these last three knots may also be used as transition knots for setting up the ability to tie a clasp knot (i.e., the 2-Strand Diamond Knot). In some cases you will be instructed to tie a 4-Strand Diamond Knot around vertical cords. To do so, follow the instructions for the 4-Strand Diamond Knot, as shown on Page 50, only leave the noted vertical cords in place as you build the Diamond Knot around them.

Note: Diamond knots can be tied clockwise or counterclockwise. However, for instructability the 2-Strand Diamond Knot is shown tied in its counterclockwise orientation, and the 4-Strand Diamond Knot is shown tied in its clockwise orientation.

Special Sizing

I'm often asked how much paracord is needed to make a specific length of a given tie (e.g., "How much cord do I need to make a 16 inch long Twist-Stitched Solomon Bar Collar?"). Questions like these aren't as easy to answer as they first appear, because of the following:

A) Paracord purchased from varying sources has varying degrees of elasticity and thickness;

B) Each tyer has his or her own degree of tightening; and

C) Different phases of a tie utilize different lengths of cord (i.e., the beginning of a tie uses up one amount of cord per inch, and the middle of a tie uses a different amount, as does the end of a tie).

All that said, a tyer can generally determine how much paracord they'll need to make a specific length of tie by tying an inch/two centimeters of that tie,

About This Book

then untying it, and seeing how many feet/meters of cord were used. The ratio revealed becomes a means of estimating how much total paracord will be required to make the final piece.

Reproduction & Sales

To the question: "Is it okay to make and sell the fusion knots and ties presented in the *Tying It All Together* (TIAT) books and online videos?", the answer is yes. Absolutely! It is my intent that others use my knots and ties as they wish, for fundraising, profit, gifts, or otherwise. I would appreciate it if you didn't change their names, but granting this request is ultimately up to you. So don't hesitate to start a business online or anywhere else you think fusion paracord ties would be appreciated. Just promise me one thing: if your livelihood is improved to the point where you can afford to give back to your community through tithing, gifts, or donation, please do. Think of it as paying forward the gifts fusion knotting gave to you.

Snipping & Singeing

Paracord is made of nylon, and nylon is a thermoplastic (also known as a thermosoftening plastic). Put another way, nylon is a polymer that turns into a liquid when heated. During this heated state it can be molded.

When it comes to paracord ties, this molding flares the "glassed" ends of the cord, making them larger than the cinched loop holding them in place. For the most part, this change in physical state seals paracord ends until a greater (human sourced) force is applied (i.e., the flared ends are pulled through the cinched loop and/or the fused glassed ends are broken).

The following page presents the step-by-step procedure used to snip and singe the ends of all the paracord ties shown in this book.

WARNING: Children should not use shears (i.e., scissors) or lighters without adult supervision. If you're reading this, and you're not sure if this warning applies to you…it probably does. Stop, show these instructions to a competent parent or guardian, and ask for their assistance.

About This Book

How to Snip & Singe Cord Ends

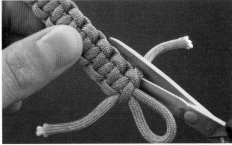

1. Begin with the possession of the following items: **Barber Shears** and a **Butane Torch Lighter**

2. Once the desired tie length is achieved, carefully snip the undesired cord ends off with your shears.

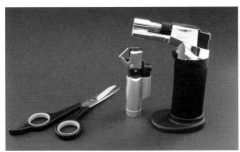

3. Once the undesired cord ends are removed…

4. …ready your lighter. Make sure to keep hands away from the lighter tip.

5. Quickly (no more than 1 to 2 seconds) singe the first snipped end of your cord…

6. …and then the second. While the "glassed" ends of your snipped paracord are still soft…

7. …but no longer hot to the touch, mold them with your thumb.

8. Congratulations, you've successfully sealed the ends of your paracord tie in place!

Twists & Terms

The following definitions and visual clarifications are meant to provide an understanding of the knotting procedures and terms associated with this book.

Definitions

ABOK: Acronym for *The Ashley Book of Knots*.

Apex: The top or highest part of an object.

Bar: A semi-rigid, tightly constructed tie typically made with square knots (e.g., Solomon Bar).

Bight: A line doubled over into a U-shape.

Bolster: The thick junction between a knife handle and its blade.

Bolt: A shaft or missile designed to be shot from a crossbow or catapult.

Bulged: To be bent outward in order to produce a rounded swelling.

Bushcraft: Wilderness survival skills that enable one to thrive in the natural environment.

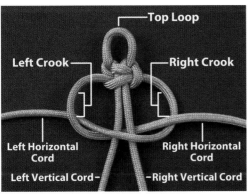

Cord Parts

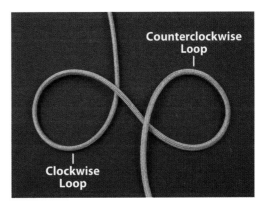

Cord Loops

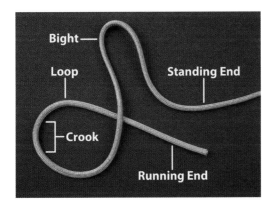

Tie Parts

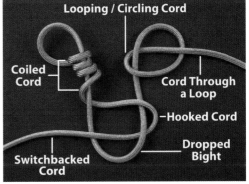

Tie Movements

Twists & Terms

Circle: A line making one complete revolution around another line or body part (e.g., finger).

Clockwise Loop: A loop that has a running end (or line on top) that rotates clockwise.

Coil: A line that makes several (more than one) revolutions around another line or body part (e.g. finger).

Component Part: A knot element or knotting technique used to make a fusion knot or tie.

Concentric: Denoting circles, arcs, or other shapes that share the same center.

Cord: A slender length of flexible material used to make a knot or tie.

Counterclockwise Loop: A loop that has a running end (or line on top) that rotates counterclockwise.

Crook: The curved inside part of a bight, circle, loop, or hooked line.

DFK: Acronym for the book *Decorative Fusion Knots*.

Ferro Rod: A man-made metallic material that produces hot sparks when scraped against a rough surface.

Firm: The point at which the adjusting of a knot results in a satisfactory appearance.

Firmly Tightening: Tightening until the knot or tie is as tight as one can make it.

Fistload: An object gripped in the hand that increases the mass of the fist and so the force of a punch.

Flip: Turning a knot, tie, or semi-completed knot or tie, over, upside down, vertically, or horizontally.

Fusion Tie: An innovative tie created through the merging of different knot elements or knotting techniques.

Hexagonal: Pertaining to a hexagon or an object with six straight sides and angles.

Historical Knot: A knot (or tie) that was discovered or created before 1979 (the year the IGKT updated ABOK).

Hook: A line that makes a sharp curve or a shape resembling a hook, typically around a line.

Horizontal: Referring to a flat or level position.

IGKT: Acronym for the International Guild of Knot Tyers.

Key Fob: A generally decorative, at times useful, item or tie that connects to a key ring or key.

Lace: A threaded cord used to tie together opposite ends.

Legs: Dangling or vertical parallel cords.

Line: The material used to tie a knot or tie (e.g., paracord, rope, wire, etc.).

Twists & Terms

Lock: To fasten or secure something in place.

Loop: A circle of line that crosses itself or a bight cinched at its base.

P: A line that is looped to look like the letter P or the mirror image of the letter P.

Paracord: A lightweight nylon rope constructed with a core of yarns wrapped in a woven exterior sheath.

Parallel: Two straight lines or cords maintaining an equal distance from one another.

PFT-V1: Acronym for the book *Paracord Fusion Ties - Volume 1*.

PFT-V2: Acronym for the book *Paracord Fusion Ties - Volume 2*.

Piece: The partially completed or final version of an entire knot or tie.

Pommel: A rounded knob on the end of a sword, machete, or dagger.

Practical Paracord Objects: Paracord ties designed to provide benefits to those who tie them, in real time; as opposed to when they are unraveled and the cord within them utilized.

Rapid Deployment Tie: A tie that transitions from its stored form to a useful length of cord quickly and easily.

Running End: The end of a line that is being used to make the knot or tie.

Singe: Scorching the end of a cut line to hold it in place or keep it from fraying.

Sinnet: A weaving technique or tie generally performed with a series of slip knots, used to shorten the length of a line.

Standing End: The end of a line that is not involved in making the knot or tie.

Tactical: Relating to, or constituting, tactics or a strategy carefully planned to achieve a specific end.

TIAT: Acronym for the YouTube video channel *Tying It All Together*.

Tuck: Inserting a line or bight through a loop or under another line.

Vertical: Referring to an upright position, at a right angle to the horizon.

Weave: Passing a line over and under another line.

X: Two lines or sets of lines that cross over one another in the configuration of the letter X.

Chapter 1

Innovative Zipper Sinnets

ZIPPER SINNET

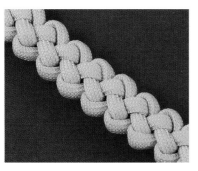

The Zipper Sinnet is one of the first ties I ever learned. Its name comes from the fact that it can be "zipped apart" whenever the cord that created it is once again required. This fact effectively makes all Zipper Sinnets rapid deployment ties.

Cord Used: *One 7 ft. (2.1 m) Cord = 7.5 in. (19.1 cm) Bracelet*

Component Parts: *Historical Knot*

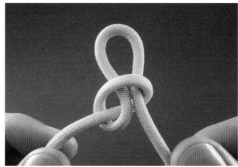

1. At the middle of the cord, make a clockwise loop.

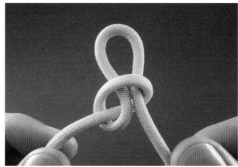

2. Bight the right running end through the loop…

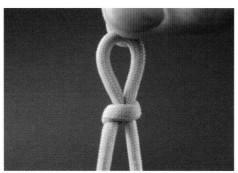

3. …and tighten, leaving a 0.5 in. (1.3 cm) loop in the Slip Knot made.

4. Flip the piece over, upside down.

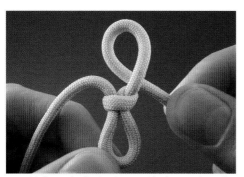

5. Make a clockwise loop with the cord on the right.

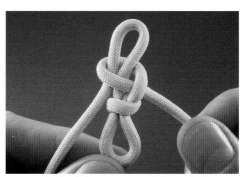

6. Bight the left running end through the right loop…

7. …and tighten, leaving a 0.5 in. (1.3 cm) loop in the Slip Knot made.

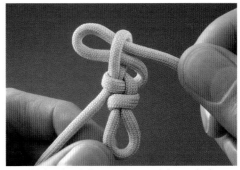

8. Bight the right running end through the left loop…

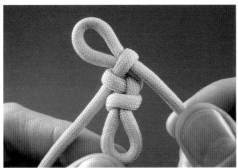

9. …and tighten, leaving a 0.5 in. (1.3 cm) loop in the Slip Knot made.

10. Repeat Steps 6 through 9 until a minimum 5 in. (12.7 cm) of cord ends remain.

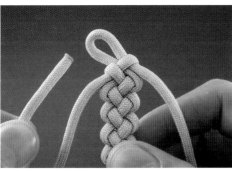

11. To lock the piece in place, take the tip of the left running end in hand.

12. Insert it through the right loop.

13. Then pull the right running end firmly.

14. Flip the piece over, upside down.

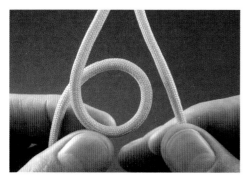

15. **2-Strand Diamond Knot:** Make a clockwise **P** with the left cord.

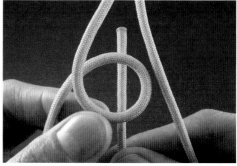

16. Lift the right running end up, behind the loop of the **P**.

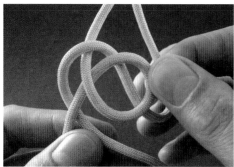

17. Drop the running end down, over the cord above the **P**, and under the "leg" of the **P**.

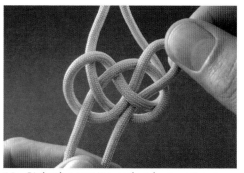

18. Bight the running end and weave it over, under, and over the cords to the right.

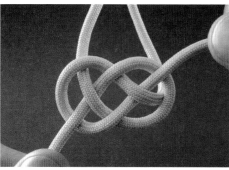

19. Pull the bight out to form a Carrick Bend.

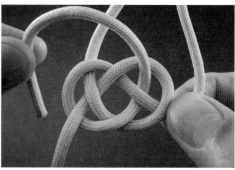

20. Now, hook the right running end left, over the (left) cord above the Carrick Bend…

21. …and insert it through the (back) center of the Carrick Bend.

22. Then hook the left running end right, over the (right) cord above the Carrick Bend…

23. …and insert it through the (back) center of the Carrick Bend.

24. Adjust the cord ends until the 2-Strand Diamond Knot is firm and symmetrical.

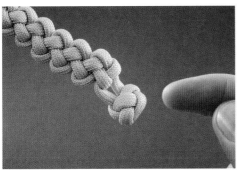

25. Carefully snip and singe the Diamond Knot ends.

26. The completed Zipper Sinnet Bracelet.

THICK ZIPPER SINNET

The Thick Zipper Sinnet is a doubling of a standard Zipper Sinnet. Holding twice as much cord as its namesake, the tie has a unique look that stretches and expands (even when wet), making it an ideal design for a bracelet.

Cord Used: *Two 7 ft. (2.1 m) Cords = 7.5 in. (19.1 cm) Bracelet*

Component Parts: *Zipper Sinnet + Doubled Contrasting Cords*

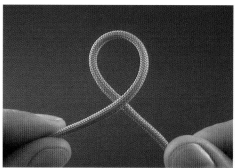

1. At the middle of the first cord, make a clockwise loop.

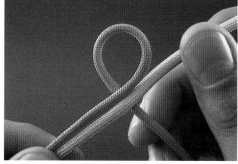

2. Then cross the middle of the second cord across the apex of the right running end.

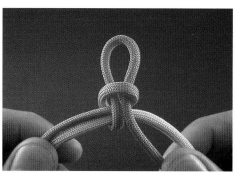

3. Bight the right running end over the second cord and through the loop.

4. Tighten the piece, leaving a 0.5 in. (1.3 cm) loop in the Slip Knot made.

5. Flip the piece over, upside down.

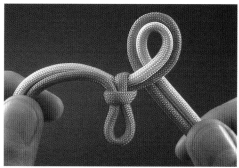

6. Make two concentric clockwise loops with the cords on the right.

7. Bight the left running ends through the right loops…

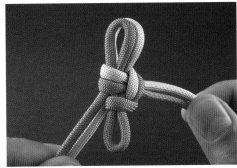

8. …and tighten, leaving two stacked 0.5 in. (1.3 cm) loops in the Slip Knots made.

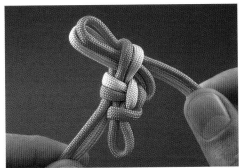

9. Bight the right running ends through the left loops…

10. …and tighten, leaving two stacked 0.5 in. (1.3 cm) loops in the Slip Knots made.

11. Repeat Steps 7 through 10 until a minimum 5 in. (12.7 cm) of cord ends remain.

12. To lock the piece in place, take the tip of the top left running end in hand.

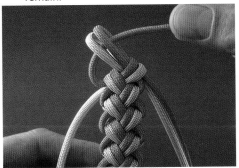

13. Insert it through the right loops.

14. Then split apart the cords below the right loops…

15. …and bulge up the two (back) parallel cords between them.

16. Take the tip of the lower left running end in hand…

17. …and insert it through the bulged cords.

18. Then pull the right running ends firmly.

19. Carefully snip and singe the right running ends, at their base.

20. Tie a 2-Strand Diamond Knot (see Page 4) with the remaining vertical cords.

21. Carefully snip and singe the Diamond Knot ends.

22. The completed Thick Zipper Sinnet Bracelet.

GENOESE ZIPPER SINNET

The Genoese Zipper Sinnet was inspired by the tiered overlapping Half Hitches of the Single Genoese Bar (see DFK). Replacing the Half Hitches with overlapping Zipper Sinnets, the tie generates a seemingly complex interwoven stitch.

Cord Used: *Two 6 ft. (1.8 m) Cords = 7.5 in. (19.1 cm) Bracelet*

Component Parts: *Zipper Sinnet + Tiered Overlapping Cords + Divided Contrasting Cords*

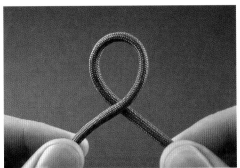

1. At the middle of the first cord, make a clockwise loop.

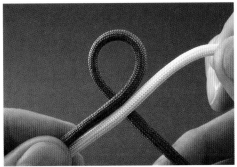

2. Then cross the middle of the second cord across the apex of the right running end.

3. Bight the right running end over the second cord and through the loop.

4. Tighten the piece, leaving a 0.5 in. (1.3 cm) loop in the Slip Knot made.

5. Flip the piece over, upside down.

6. Pull the ends of the first and second cords apart, to the left and right, respectively.

7. Make a clockwise loop with the top cord on the right.

8. Bight the leftmost running end through the right loop…

9. …and tighten, leaving a 0.5 in. (1.3 cm) loop in the Slip Knot made.

10. Bight the lower right running end over the cord above it, through the left loop…

11. …and tighten, leaving a 0.5 in. (1.3 cm) loop in the Slip Knot made.

12. Bight the lower left running end over the cord above it, through the right loop…

13. …and tighten, leaving a 0.5 in. (1.3 cm) loop in the Slip Knot made.

14. Repeat Steps 10 through 13 until a minimum 5 in. (12.7 cm) of cord ends remain.

15. To lock the piece in place, take the tip of the lower right running end in hand.

16. Pass it over the cord above it and through the left loop.

17. Then pull the top left running end firmly.

18. Carefully snip and singe the lower two running ends, at their base.

19. With the remaining vertical cords…

20. …tie a 2-Strand Diamond Knot (see Page 4).

21. Carefully snip and singe the Diamond Knot ends.

22. The completed Genoese Zipper Sinnet Bracelet.

THE RADULA

The Radula mimics the appearance of the minutely toothed ribbon mollusks use for feeding. Essentially an integrated contrasting cord version of the Genoese Zipper Sinnet, the tie illustrates the massive impact a subtle design shift can make.

Cord Used: *Two 6 ft. (1.8 m) Cords = 7.5 in. (19.1 cm) Bracelet*

Component Parts: *Zipper Sinnet + Tiered Overlapping Cords + Integrated Contrasting Cords*

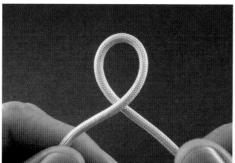

1. At the middle of the first cord, make a clockwise loop.

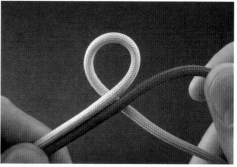

2. Then cross the middle of the second cord across the apex of the right running end.

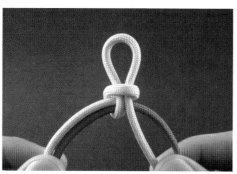

3. Bight the right running end over the second cord and through the loop.

4. Tighten the piece, leaving a 0.5 in. (1.3 cm) loop in the Slip Knot made.

5. Flip the piece over, upside down.

6. Make a clockwise loop with the front cord on the right.

7. Bight the back left running end through the right loop…

8. …and tighten, leaving a 0.5 in. (1.3 cm) loop in the Slip Knot made.

9. Bight the lower right running end over the cord above it, through the left loop…

10. …and tighten, leaving a 0.5 in. (1.3 cm) loop in the Slip Knot made.

11. Bight the lower left running end over the cord above it, through the right loop…

12. …and tighten, leaving a 0.5 in. (1.3 cm) loop in the Slip Knot made.

13. Bight the lower right running end over the cord above it, through the left loop…

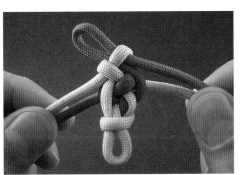

14. …and tighten, leaving a 0.5 in. (1.3 cm) loop in the Slip Knot made.

15. Bight the lower left running end over the cord above it, through the right loop…

16. …and tighten, leaving a 0.5 in. (1.3 cm) loop in the Slip Knot made.

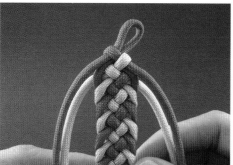

17. Repeat Steps 9 through 16 until a minimum 5 in. (12.7 cm) of cord ends remain.

18. To lock the piece in place, take the tip of the lower right running end in hand.

19. Pass it over the cord above it and through the left loop.

20. Then pull the top left running end firmly.

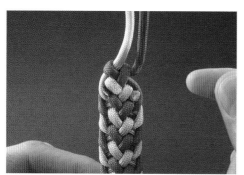

21. Carefully snip and singe the lower two running ends, at their base.

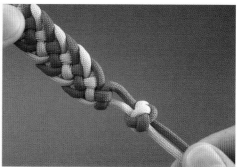

22. Tie a 2-Strand Diamond Knot (see Page 4) with the remaining vertical cords.

23. Carefully snip and singe the Diamond Knot ends.

24. The completed Radula Bracelet.

Mystic Zipper Sinnet

The Mystic Zipper Sinnet is a sneaky way to incorporate a flash of color into an otherwise standard Zipper Sinnet. The end product confounds most, creating the illusion of a second cord appearing from nowhere.

Cord Used: *One 6 ft. (1.8 m) Cord & One 4 ft. (1.2 m) Cord = Varying Sized Bracelet*

Component Parts: *Zipper Sinnet + Mystical Tunneling Technique + Integrated Contrasting Cords*

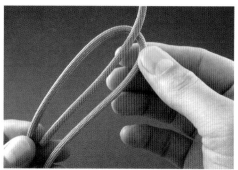

1. Five in. (13 cm) up behind the bottom of the short cord, bight the middle of the long cord.

2. Hook its left running end right, creating a counterclockwise loop around the short cord.

3. Bight the right running end through the loop…

4. …and tighten, leaving a 0.5 in. (1.3 cm) loop in the Slip Knot made.

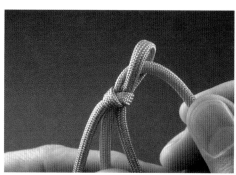

5. Insert the short cord through the right loop.

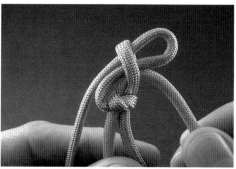

6. Bight the left running end through the right loop (over the inserted cord)…

7. …and tighten, leaving a 0.5 in. (1.3 cm) loop in the Slip Knot made.

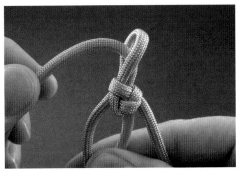

8. Insert the short cord through the left loop.

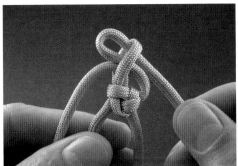

9. Bight the right running end through the left loop (over the inserted cord)…

10. …and tighten, leaving a 0.5 in. (1.3 cm) loop in the Slip Knot made.

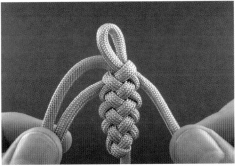

11. Repeat Steps 5 through 10 three more times.

12. Insert the left running end through the right loop.

13. Bight the short cord through the right loop (over the inserted cord)…

14. …and tighten, leaving a 0.5 in. (1.3 cm) loop in the Slip Knot made.

15. Insert the upper right cord through the left loop.

16. Bight the right running end through the left loop (over the inserted cord)…

17. …and tighten, leaving a 0.5 in. (1.3 cm) loop in the Slip Knot made.

18. Repeat Steps 12 through 17 three more times.

19. Then repeat Steps 5 through 10 and Steps 12 through 17, until a minimum 5 in. (12.7 cm) of the short cord remain.

20. Insert the short cord through the right loop.

21. Pull the left and then the right running ends firmly.

22. Carefully snip and singe the two running ends, at their base.

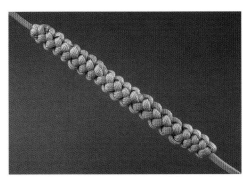

23. At this point, you've successfully made a Mystic Zipper Sinnet.

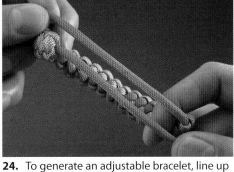

24. To generate an adjustable bracelet, line up the short cord ends.

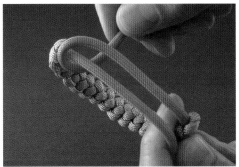

25. Circle the right cord end around the left cord and itself.

26. Then insert the cord end through the loop. Tighten the Overhand Knot made, firmly.

27. Flip the piece over, upside down, and repeat Steps 24 through 26.

28. To finish the bracelet carefully snip and singe the Overhand Knot ends 0.25 in. (~0.5 cm) from their bases.

Chapter 2

Twisted, Bumpy, & Flowing Bars

TWIST-STITCHED SOLOMON BAR

The Twist-Stitched Solomon Bar is the twisted version of the Stitched Solomon Bar (see PFT-V1). But unlike other twisted ties, this one bends into an arch instead of spiraling into a corkscrew, making it a great design for a bracelet or collar.

Cord Used: *One 7 ft. (2.1 m) Cord & One 4 ft. (1.2 m) Cord = 7.5 in. (19.1 cm) Bracelet*

Component Parts: *Stitched Solomon Bar + Left Split Weaves + Contrasting Cords*

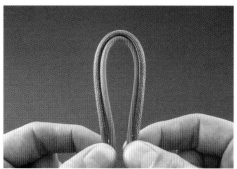

1. Start with bights created at the middle of the two cords.

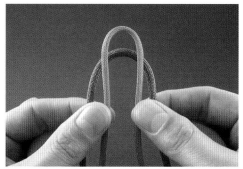

2. Drop the long cord down 0.5 in. (1.3 cm), behind the bight of the short cord.

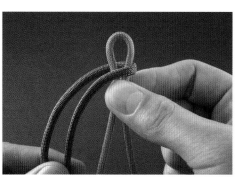

3. Hook the right running end left, over the vertical cords.

4. Drop the left running end over the cord beneath it.

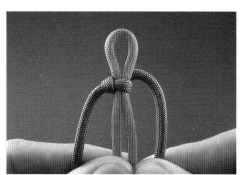

5. Then hook it right, under the vertical cords, and through the back of the right crook. Tighten firmly.

6. Weave the right running end left, under, and over the vertical cords.

7. Drop the left running end over the cord beneath it.

8. Then hook it right, under the vertical cords, and through the back of the right crook. Tighten firmly.

9. Weave the right running end left, over, and under the vertical cords.

10. Drop the left running end under the cord beneath it.

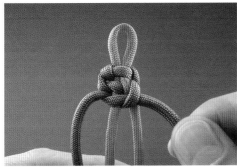

11. Then hook it right, over the vertical cords, and through the front of the right crook. Tighten firmly.

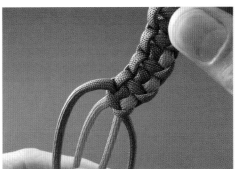

12. Repeat Steps 6 through 11 until a minimum 5 in. (12.7 cm) of cord ends remain.

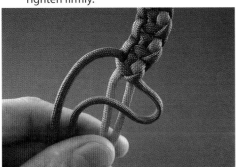

13. Now, hook the right running end left, over the vertical cords.

14. Drop the left running end over the cord beneath it.

15. Then hook it right, under the vertical cords, and through the back of the right crook. Tighten firmly.

16. Carefully snip and singe the horizontal cord ends, at their base.

17. Tie a 2-Strand Diamond Knot (see Page 4) with the vertical cords.

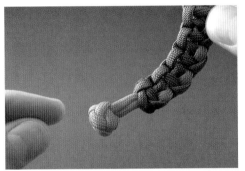

18. Carefully snip and singe the Diamond Knot ends.

19. Note: The bar is supposed to arch.

20. The completed Twist-Stitched Solomon Bar Bracelet.

SECRET RIVER BAR

The Secret River Bar is the fusion of a Solomon Bar and a subtle modification of the Desert Flower Medallion tying technique. Together, these two ties make something very different, a convex bar with a meandering "river" of cord flowing down its middle.

Cord Used: *One 6 ft. (1.8 m) Cord & One 5 ft. (1.5 m) Cord = 7.5 in. (19.1 cm) Bracelet*

Component Parts: *Solomon Bar + Left-Right Single Cord Loops + Integrated Contrasting Cords*

1. Start with bights created at the middle of the two cords.

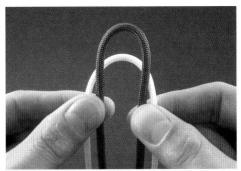

2. Drop the long cord down 0.5 in. (1.3 cm), behind the bight of the short cord.

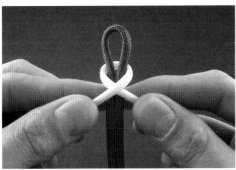

3. Cross the back cords over the front (vertical) cords, right over left.

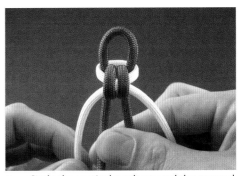

4. Circle the vertical cords around the crossed cords, between the legs above.

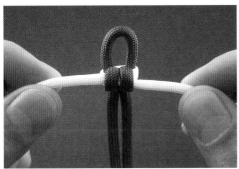

5. Tighten the piece until firm, leaving a 0.5 in. (1.3 cm) bight on top.

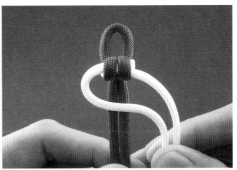

6. Hook the left running end right, over the vertical cords.

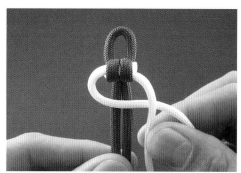

7. Drop the right running end over the cord beneath it.

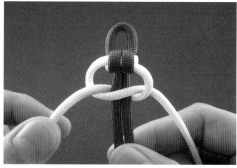

8. Then hook it left, under the vertical cords, and through the back of the left crook.

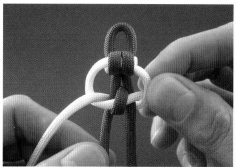

9. Circle the left vertical cord around both horizontal cords (front and back), between the legs above.

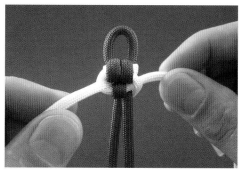

10. Adjust the cords until the piece is firm.

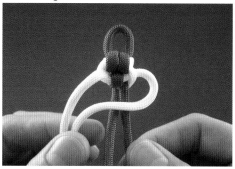

11. Hook the right running end left, over the vertical cords.

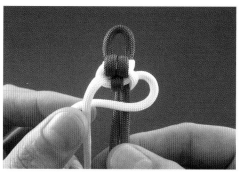

12. Drop the left running end over the cord beneath it.

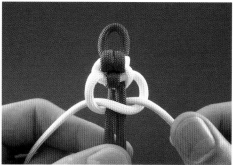

13. Then hook it right, under the vertical cords, and through the back of the right crook.

14. Circle the right vertical cord around both horizontal cords (front and back), between the legs above.

15. Adjust the cords until the piece is firm.

16. Repeat Steps 6 through 15 until a minimum 5 in. (12.7 cm) of cord ends remain.

17. Now, hook the left running end right, over the vertical cords.

18. Drop the right running end over the cord beneath it.

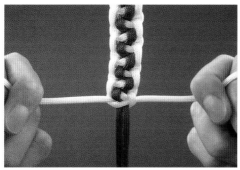

19. Then hook it left, under the vertical cords, and through the back of the left crook. Tighten firmly.

20. Carefully snip and singe the horizontal cord ends, at their base.

21. Tie a 2-Strand Diamond Knot (see Page 4) with the vertical cords.

22. Carefully snip and singe the Diamond Knot ends.

23. Flip the piece over, horizontally, to see the "secret river" side.

24. The completed Secret River Bar Bracelet.

CROOKED RIVER BAR

The Crooked River Bar's name derives from the fact that its front looks like a crooked river darting to and fro between rock-lined banks. Beyond its dynamic look, the tying technique generates a sturdy bar that makes an excellent bracelet.

Cord Used: *Two 5 ft. (1.5 m) Cords = 7.5 in. (19.1 cm) Bracelet*

Component Parts: *Cross-Locked Bights + Overhand Knots + Integrated Contrasting Cords*

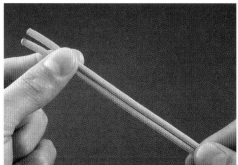

1. Draw the two cords out side-by-side the length of the desired bracelet, plus (+) 5 in. (12.7 cm).

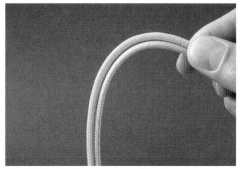

2. With the short cord ends facing down, on the left…

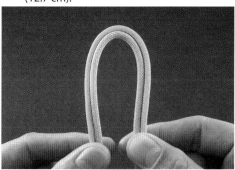

3. …bight the long cord ends to the right, at the measured point (see Step 1).

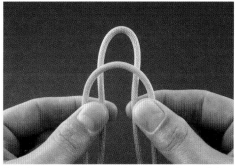

4. Drop one of the cords down in front of the bight of the other.

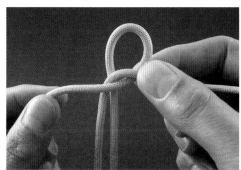

5. Hook the right running end of the back cord left, over the vertical cords to the left.

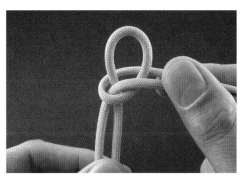

6. Then hook the running end right, around the back of the top loop…

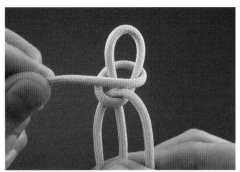

7. …left around the front of the loop…

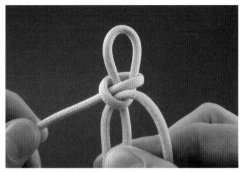

8. …and through the left crook, making a "loop around a loop" or a Slip Knot.

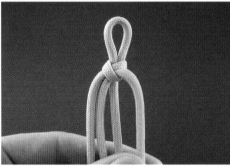

9. Tighten the piece until firm, leaving a 0.5 in. (1.3 cm) loop on top.

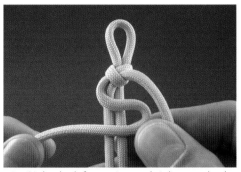

10. Bight the left running end right, over both vertical cords.

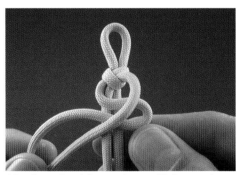

11. Cross the right running end left, over the bight and the vertical cords beneath it.

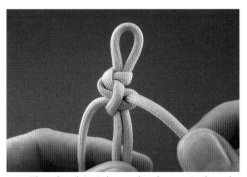

12. Then hook it right, under the vertical cords, and through the back of the bight's right crook. Tighten firmly.

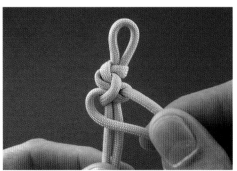

13. Hook the left running end right, over the vertical cords.

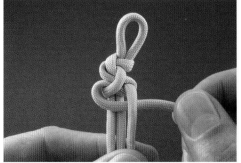

14. Drop the right running end over the cord beneath it.

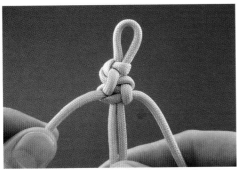

15. Then hook it left, under the vertical cords, and through the back of the left crook. Tighten firmly.

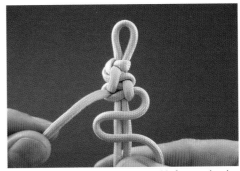

16. Bight the right running end left, over both vertical cords.

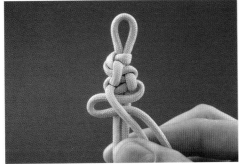

17. Cross the left running end right, over the bight and the vertical cords beneath it.

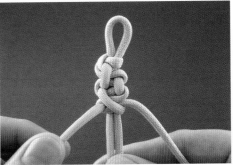

18. Then hook it left, under the vertical cords, and through the back of the bight's left crook. Tighten firmly.

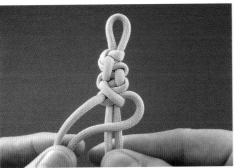

19. Hook the right running end left, over the vertical cords.

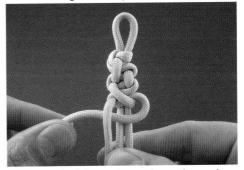

20. Drop the left running end over the cord beneath it.

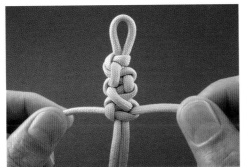

21. Then hook it right, under the vertical cords, and through the back of the right crook. Tighten firmly.

22. Repeat Steps 10 through 21 until a minimum 5 in. (12.7 cm) of cord ends remain.

23. Carefully snip and singe the horizontal cord ends, at their base.

24. Tie a 2-Strand Diamond Knot (see Page 4) with the vertical cords.

25. Carefully snip and singe the Diamond Knot ends.

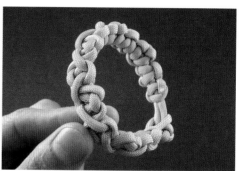

26. The completed Crooked River Bar Bracelet.

COBBLED SOLOMON BAR

The Cobbled Solomon Bar is another unique take on the classic Solomon Bar. Incorporating a circling technique prior to each Square Knot tied, the piece doesn't seem like much at first. That is, until you flip it over, revealing its perplexing cobbled side.

Cord Used: *One 6 ft. (1.8 m) Cord & One 5 ft. (1.5 m) Cord = 7.5 in. (19.1 cm) Bracelet*

Component Parts: *Solomon Bar + Circled Cords + Integrated Contrasting Cords*

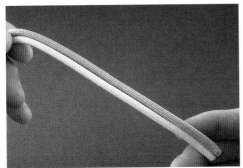

1. Draw the two cords out side-by-side the length of the desired bracelet, plus (+) 5 in. (12.7 cm), long cord on the right.

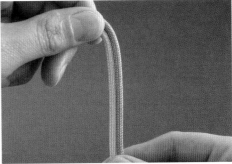

2. With the short cord ends facing down, grip the measured point (see Step 1).

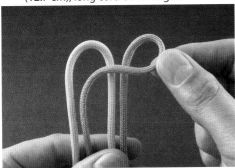

3. Now, hook the right running end left, over the vertical cords.

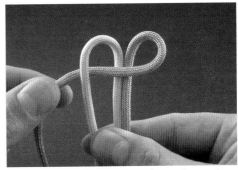

4. Drop the left running end over the cord beneath it.

5. Then hook it right and through the back of the right loop.

6. Insert the right running end through the front of the left loop.

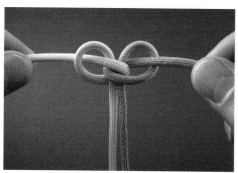

7. Insert the left running end through the back of the right loop.

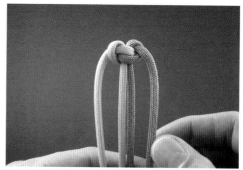

8. Adjust the cords until the piece is firm.

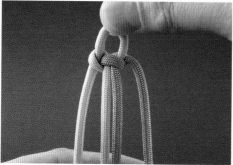

9. Pull the top cord up to make a 0.5 in. (1.3 cm) bight.

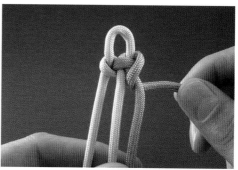

10. Circle the right running end around the front of the vertical cord to its left.

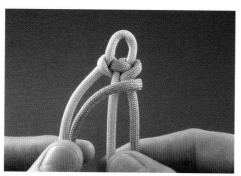

11. Then hook it left, over the vertical cords.

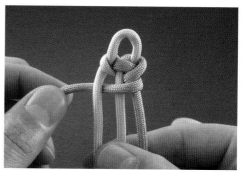

12. Drop the left running end over the cord beneath it.

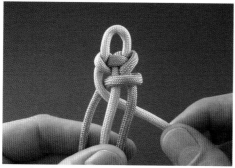

13. Then hook it right, under the vertical cords.

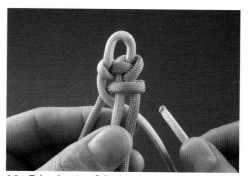

14. Take the tip of the hooked cord in hand…

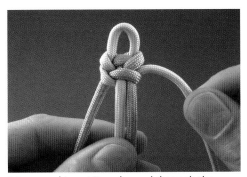

15. …and insert it under and through the crook of the right cord above. Tighten firmly.

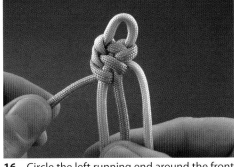

16. Circle the left running end around the front of the vertical cord to its right.

17. Then hook it right, over the vertical cords.

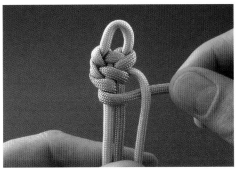

18. Drop the right running end over the cord beneath it.

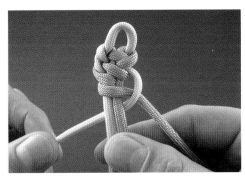

19. Then hook it left, under the vertical cords.

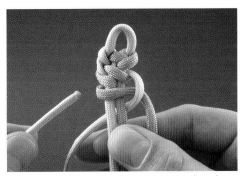

20. Take the tip of the hooked cord in hand…

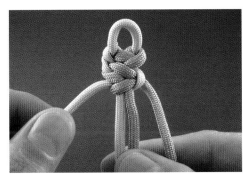

21. …and insert it under and through the crook of the left cord above. Tighten firmly.

22. Repeat Steps 10 through 21 until a minimum 5 in. (12.7 cm) of cord ends remain.

23. Carefully snip and singe the horizontal cord ends, at their base—cobbled side showing.

24. Tie a 2-Strand Diamond Knot (see Page 4) with the vertical cords.

25. Carefully snip and singe the Diamond Knot ends.

26. The completed Cobbled Solomon Bar Bracelet.

SURREAL SOLOMON BAR

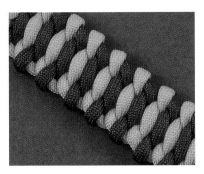

The Surreal Solomon Bar is a relatively easy way to make a lateral version of a Tire Tread Bar (see PFT-V1). That is to say, instead of the "ribs" of the bar slanting, they lie parallel to one another. Sturdy and rugged looking, the tie makes a nice bracelet or strap for a bag.

Cord Used: *Two 6 ft. (1.8 m) Cords = 7.5 in. (19.1 cm) Bracelet*

Component Parts: *Solomon Bar + Hooked Cords + Integrated Contrasting Cords*

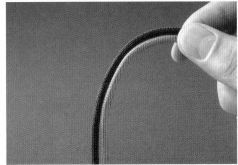

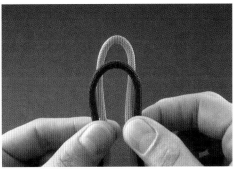

1. Draw the two cords out side-by-side the length of the desired bracelet, plus (+) 5 in. (12.7 cm).

2. With the short cord ends facing down, on the left…

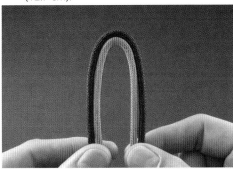

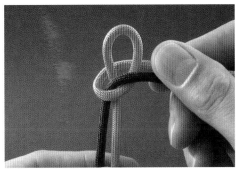

3. …bight the long cord ends to the right, at the measured point (See Step 1).

4. Drop one of the cords down in front of the bight of the other.

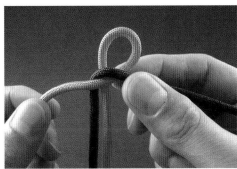

5. Hook the right running end of the back cord left, over the vertical cords to the left.

6. Then hook the running end right, around the back of the top loop…

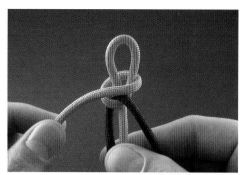

7.   …left around the front of the loop…

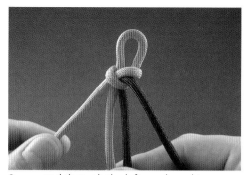

8.   …and through the left crook, making a "loop around a loop" or a Slip Knot.

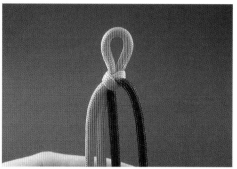

9.   Tighten the piece until firm, leaving a 0.5 in. (1.3 cm) loop on top, with the cords oriented as shown.

10.   Hook the right running end left, under the vertical cords.

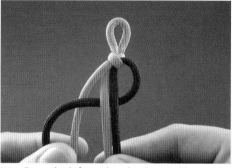

11.   Drop the left cord under the cord beneath it.

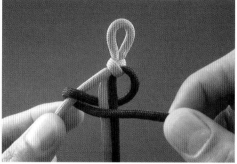

12.   Then hook the running end around the back of the left cord, over the vertical cords…

13.   …and through the front of the right crook.

14.   Adjust the cords until the "rib" is firm.

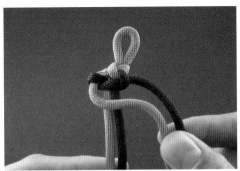

15. Hook the left running end right, over the vertical cords.

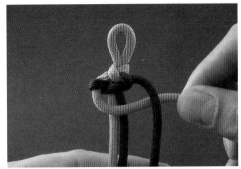

16. Drop the right cord over the cord beneath it.

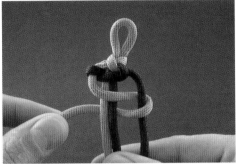

17. Then hook the running end around the front of the right cord, under the vertical cords…

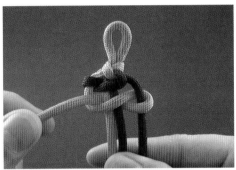

18. …and through the back of the left crook.

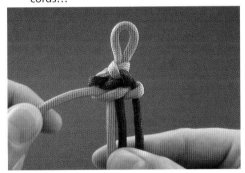

19. Adjust the cords until the "rib" is firm.

20. Repeat Steps 10 through 19 until a minimum 5 in. (12.7 cm) of cord ends remain.

21. Hook the left running end right, under the vertical cords.

22. Drop the right cord under the cord beneath it.

23. Then hook it left, over the vertical cords, and through the front of the right crook.

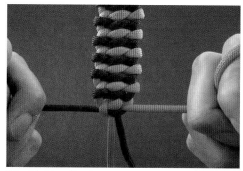

24. Tighten firmly.

25. Carefully snip and singe the horizontal cord ends, at their base.

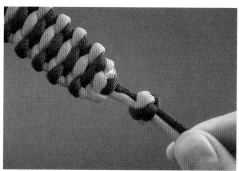

26. Tie a 2-Strand Diamond Knot (see Page 4) with the vertical cords.

27. Carefully snip and singe the Diamond Knot ends.

28. The completed Surreal Solomon Bar Bracelet.

Chapter 3

Coronation of Crown Sinnets

ROUND CROWN SINNET

Despite its common name, the Round Crown Sinnet is actually a cylinder. Still, don't let this fact stop you from enjoying its creation. Not only does the Round Crown Sinnet lend itself well to a key fob, it also makes a nice luggage marker or zipper pull.

Cord Used: *Two 5 ft. (1.5 m) Cords = 3.5 in. (8.9 cm) Key Fob*

Component Parts: *Historical Knot*

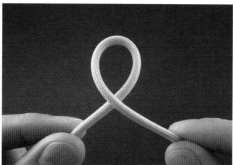

1. At the middle of the first cord, make a counterclockwise loop.

2. Lace the second cord through the loop, until its middle is reached.

3. Flip the piece over, vertically, slide your forefinger into the loop, and extend the second cord laterally.

4. Arch the second cord ends over the first, in opposite directions, right cord above left.

5. Weave the lower cord end over the arch above it…

6. …and through the crook of the second arch.

7. Weave the upper cord end over the arch below it…

8. …and through the crook of the second arch. Tighten the Crown Knot made, firmly.

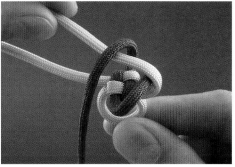

9. Arch the right and left cord ends over the cords below, in opposite directions, right cord above left.

10. Weave the lower cord end over the arch above it and through the crook of the second arch.

11. Weave the upper cord end over the arch below it and through the crook of the second arch. Tighten the knot firmly.

12. Repeat Steps 9 through 11 until a minimum 5 in. (12.7 cm) of cord ends remain.

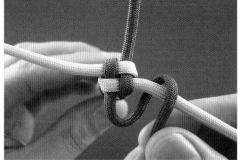

13. Wall Knot (Collapsed): Moving counterclockwise, hook the bottom cord end under and around the right cord end.

14. Hook the right cord end under and around the top cord end.

15. Hook the top cord end under and around the left cord end.

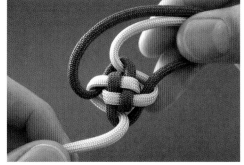

16. Then insert the left cord end under and through the bottom crook.

17. Tighten the Wall Knot made, firmly.

18. To lock the Wall Knot in place, push it down, collapsing it forward…

19. …while pulling down on the vertical cords beneath it.

20. Carefully snip and singe the cord ends to complete the Round Crown Sinnet Fob.

ROYAL CROWN SINNET

The Royal Crown Sinnet is the product of Crown Knots and Wall Knots stacked on top of one another. Thicker than most 4-strand sinnets, the tie's interlocking parallel lines are accentuated by the contrasting cords used.

Cord Used: *Two 6 ft. (1.8 m) Cords = 3.5 in. (8.9 cm) Key Fob*

Component Parts: *Crown Knots + Wall Knots (Uncollapsed) + Contrasting Cords*

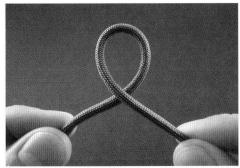

1. At the middle of the first cord, make a counterclockwise loop.

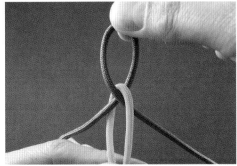

2. Lace the second cord through the loop, until its middle is reached.

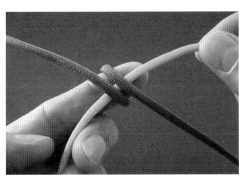

3. Flip the piece over, vertically, slide your forefinger into the loop, and extend the second cord laterally.

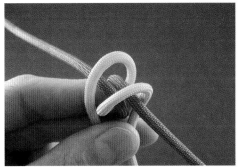

4. Arch the second cord ends over the first, in opposite directions, right cord above left.

5. Weave the lower cord end over the arch above it…

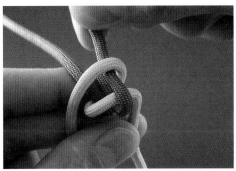

6. …and through the crook of the second arch.

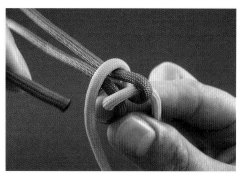

7. Weave the upper cord end over the arch below it…

8. …and through the crook of the second arch. Tighten the Crown Knot made, firmly.

9. Moving counterclockwise, hook the bottom cord end under and around the right cord end.

10. Hook the right cord end under and around the top cord end.

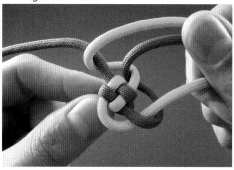

11. Hook the top cord end under and around the left cord end.

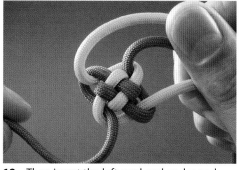

12. Then insert the left cord end under and through the bottom crook.

13. Tighten the Wall Knot made, firmly, but do not collapse it.

14. Arch the left and right cord ends over the cords below, in opposite directions, left cord above right.

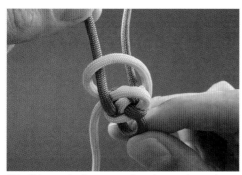

15. Weave the lower cord end over the arch above it and through the crook of the second arch.

16. Weave the upper cord end over the arch below it and through the crook of the second arch. Tighten the knot firmly.

17. Repeat Steps 9 through 16 until a minimum 5 in. (12.7 cm) of cord ends remain.

18. Tie a collapsed Wall Knot (see Page 43) with the horizontal cords.

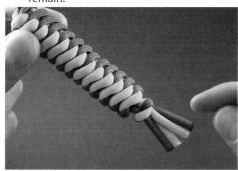

19. Carefully snip and singe the cord ends.

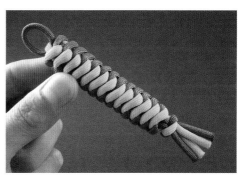

20. The completed Royal Crown Sinnet Fob.

CORKSCREW CROWN SINNET

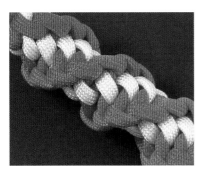

The Corkscrew Crown Sinnet is an innovative way to create a thick corkscrew pattern off the base of a Crown Knot. Above and beyond the tying technique's newness, its eye-catching twist will confound all paracorders not in the know.

Cord Used: *Two 6 ft. (1.8 m) Cords = 3.5 in. (8.9 cm) Key Fob*

Component Parts: *Oblong Crown Sinnet + Corkscrew Version + Contrasting Cords*

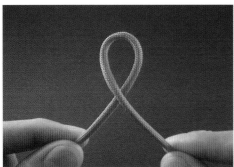

1. At the middle of the first cord, make a counterclockwise loop.

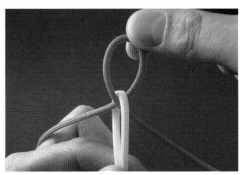

2. Lace the second cord through the loop, until its middle is reached.

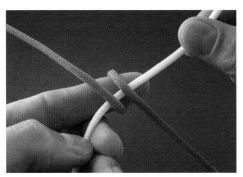

3. Flip the piece over, vertically, slide your forefinger into the loop, and extend the second cord laterally.

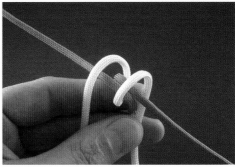

4. Arch the second cord ends over the first, in opposite directions, right cord above left.

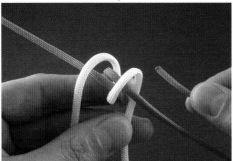

5. Weave the lower cord end over the arch above it…

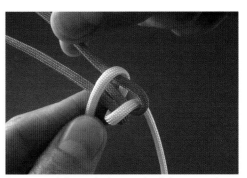

6. …and through the crook of the second arch.

7. Weave the upper cord end over the arch below it…

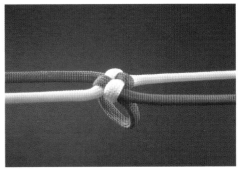

8. …and through the crook of the second arch. Tighten the Crown Knot made, firmly.

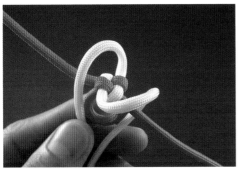

9. Arch the right and left cord ends over the cords below, in opposite directions, right cord above left.

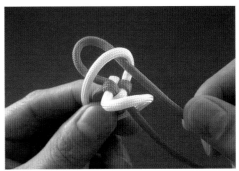

10. Weave the upper cord end through the crook of the arch below it and over the second arch.

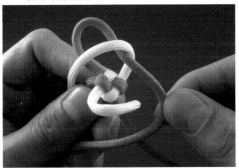

11. Then hook the cord end left over the lower cord end.

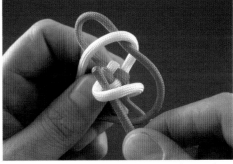

12. Weave the lower cord end over the cord above it, through the crook of the first arch…

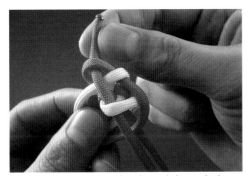

13. …over the second arch, and through the crook on top.

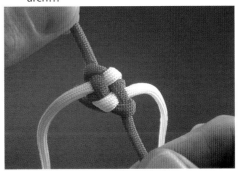

14. Adjust the cords until the knot is firm.

15. Repeat Steps 9 through 14 until a minimum 5 in. (12.7 cm) of cord ends remain.

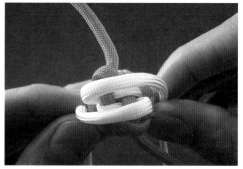

16. **4-Strand Diamond Knot:** Arch the left and right cord ends over the cords below, in opposite directions, left cord above right.

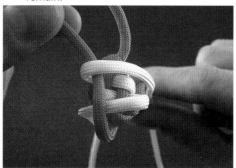

17. Weave the lower cord end over the arch above it and through the crook of the second arch.

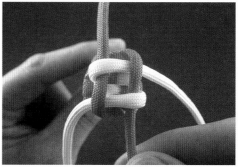

18. Weave the upper cord end over the arch below it and through the crook of the second arch.

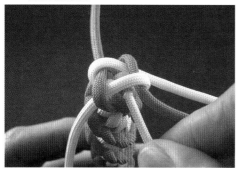

19. Now, hook the right cord end clockwise, around the arched cord beside it…

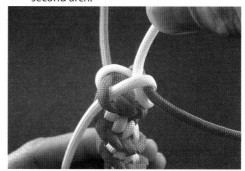

20. …and insert it through the center of the Crown Knot.

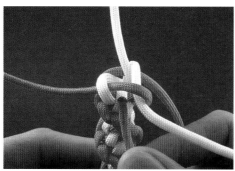

21. Hook the next cord end (in front of the one before) clockwise, around the arched cord beside it…

22. …and insert it through the center of the Crown Knot.

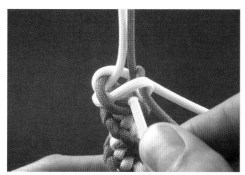

23. Hook the next cord end (in front of the one before) clockwise, around the arched cord beside it…

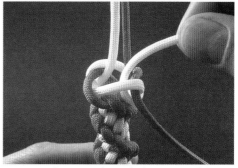

24. …and insert it through the center of the Crown Knot.

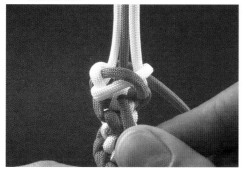

25. Finally, hook the last cord end clockwise, around the arched cord beside it…

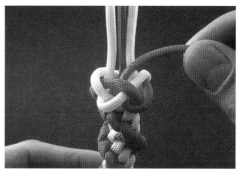

26. …and insert it through the center of the Crown Knot.

27. Adjust the vertical cords until the knot is firm and symmetrical.

28. Carefully snip and singe the cord ends to complete the Corkscrew Crown Sinnet Fob.

Striped Crown Sinnet

The Striped Crown Sinnet is the flipside of the Corkscrew Crown Sinnet. Although visually different, it's simply an alternative version of the corkscrew structure. Generating a wide tie with a clean stripe down its middle, it makes an awesome key fob.

Cord Used: *Two 6 ft. (1.8 m) Cords = 3.5 in. (8.9 cm) Key Fob*

Component Parts: *Oblong Crown Sinnet + Striped Version + Contrasting Cords*

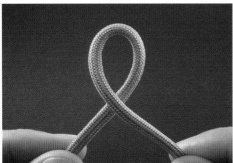

1. At the middle of the first cord, make a counterclockwise loop.

2. Lace the second cord through the loop, until its middle is reached.

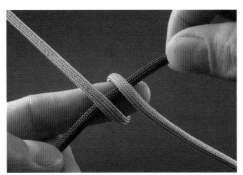

3. Flip the piece over, vertically, slide your forefinger into the loop, and extend the second cord laterally.

4. Arch the second cord ends over the first, in opposite directions, right cord above left.

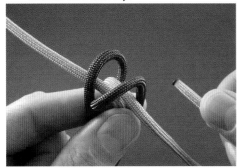

5. Weave the lower cord end over the arch above it…

6. …and through the crook of the second arch.

7. Weave the upper cord end over the arch below it…

8. …and through the crook of the second arch. Tighten the Crown Knot made, firmly.

9. Arch the left and right cord ends over the cords below, in opposite directions, left cord above right.

10. Weave the upper cord end through the crook of the arch below it and over the second arch.

11. Then hook the cord end right over the lower cord end.

12. Weave the lower cord end over the cord above it, through the crook of the first arch…

13. …over the second arch, and through the crook on top.

14. Adjust the cords until the knot is firm.

15. Arch the right and left cord ends over the cords below, in opposite directions, right cord above left.

16. Weave the upper cord end through the crook of the arch below it and over the second arch.

17. Then hook the cord end left over the lower cord end.

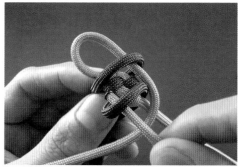

18. Weave the lower cord end over the cord above it, through the crook of the first arch…

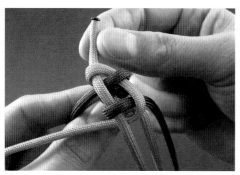

19. …over the second arch, and through the crook on top.

20. Adjust the cords until the knot is firm.

21. Repeat Steps 9 through 20 until a minimum 5 in. (12.7 cm) of cord ends remain.

22. Tie a 4-Strand Diamond Knot (see Page 50) with the horizontal cords.

23. Carefully snip and singe the cord ends.

24. The completed Striped Crown Sinnet Fob.

SPECTRALLY CLUSTERED CROWN SINNET

The Spectrally Clustered Crown Sinnet adds clustered colors to an otherwise standard Square Crown Sinnet. Although the instructions show the tying technique in three colors, it can also be made with four or even five colors, creating a customizable cascading color effect.

Cord Used: *Three 7 ft. (2.1 m) Cords = 3.5 in. (8.9 cm) Key Fob*

Component Parts: *Square Crown Sinnet + Spectrally Clustered Cords*

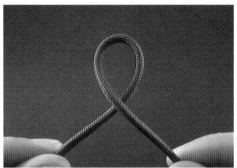

1. At the middle of the first cord, make a counterclockwise loop.

2. Lace the second and third cords through the loop, side-by-side, until their middles are reached.

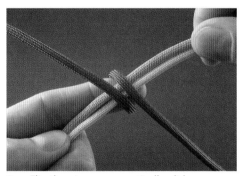

3. Flip the piece over, vertically, slide your forefinger into the loop, and extend the second and third cords laterally.

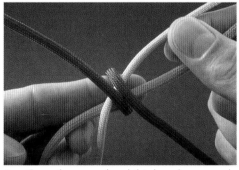

4. Cross the second and third cords over each other, making an **X**.

5. Arch the second and third cord ends over the first, in opposite directions, right cords above left.

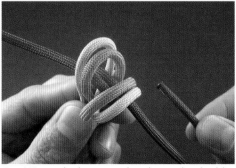

6. Weave the lower cord end over the double arches above it…

7. …and through the crooks of the second double arches.

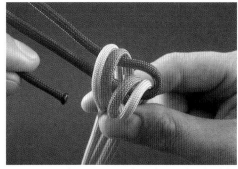

8. Weave the upper cord end over the double arches below it…

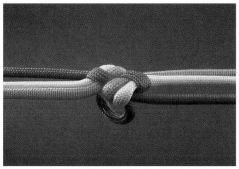

9. …and through the crooks of the second double arches. Tighten the Crown Knot made, firmly.

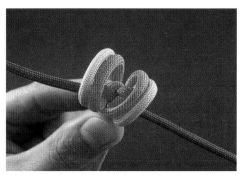

10. Arch the left and right cord ends over the cords below, in opposite directions, left cords above right.

11. Weave the upper cord end over the double arches below it and through the crooks of the second double arches.

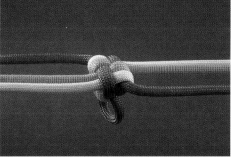

12. Weave the lower cord end over the double arches above it and through the crooks of the second double arches. Tighten firmly.

13. Arch the right and left cord ends over the cords below, in opposite directions, right cords above left.

14. Weave the lower cord end over the double arches above it and through the crooks of the second double arches.

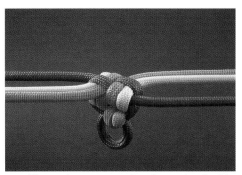

15. Weave the upper cord end over the double arches below it and through the crooks of the second double arches. Tighten firmly.

16. Repeat Steps 10 through 15 until a minimum 5 in. (12.7 cm) of cord ends remain.

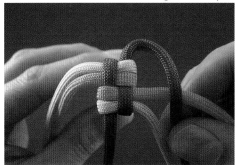

17. 6-Strand Diamond Knot: Moving clockwise, cross the top cord over the upper right cord below it.

18. Cross the upper right cord over the lower right cord below it.

19. Cross the lower right cord over the bottom cord.

20. Cross the bottom cord over the lower left cord above it.

21. Cross the lower left cord over the upper left cord above it.

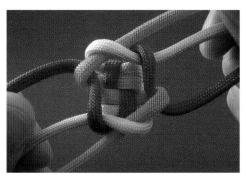

22. Then insert the upper left cord end over and through the top crook.

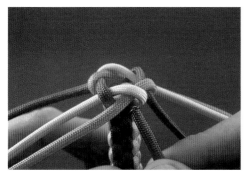

23. Now, hook the lower right cord end clockwise, around the arched cord beside it…

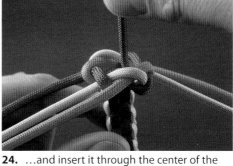

24. …and insert it through the center of the Crown Knot.

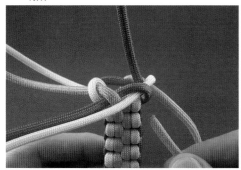

25. Hook the next cord end (in front of the one before) clockwise, around the arched cord beside it…

26. …and insert it through the center of the Crown Knot.

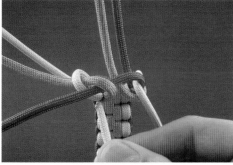

27. Hook the next cord end (in front of the one before) clockwise, around the arched cord beside it…

28. …and insert it through the center of the Crown Knot.

29. Hook the next cord end (in front of the one before) clockwise, around the arched cord beside it…

30. …and insert it through the center of the Crown Knot.

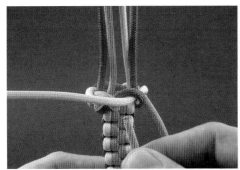

31. Hook the next cord end (in front of the one before) clockwise, around the arched cord beside it…

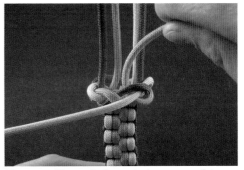

32. …and insert it through the center of the Crown Knot.

33. Finally, hook the last cord end clockwise, around the arched cord beside it…

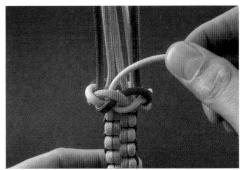

34. …and insert it through the center of the Crown Knot.

35. Adjust the vertical cords until the knot is firm and symmetrical.

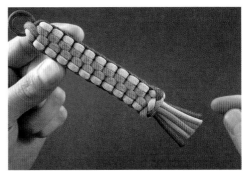

36. Carefully snip and singe the cord ends to complete the Spectrally Clustered Crown Sinnet Fob.

Chapter 4

Sine Wave
Sinnets

SINE WAVE SINNET

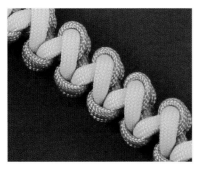

A sine wave is a waveform that exhibits smooth repetitive oscillations of a constant amplitude. The Sine Wave Sinnet mimics this waveform with cord, producing a pleasingly symmetrical zigzagging pattern that expands and contracts with a pull of the tie's ends.

Cord Used: *Two 5 ft. (1.5 m) Cords = 3.5 in. (8.9 cm) Key Fob*

Component Parts: *Sine Wave Sinnet*

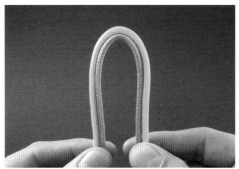

1. Start with bights created at the middle of the two cords.

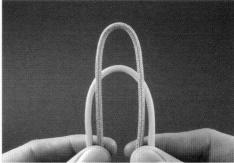

2. Drop one of the cords down 0.5 in. (1.3 cm) behind the bight of the other.

3. Cross the back cords over the front (vertical) cords, right over left.

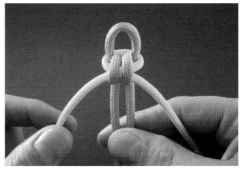

4. Circle the vertical cords around the crossed cords, between the legs above.

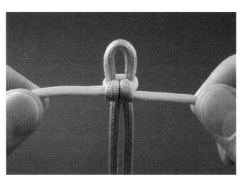

5. Tighten the piece until firm, leaving a 0.5 in. (1.3 cm) bight on top.

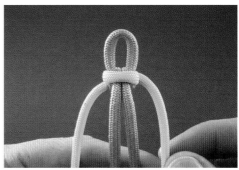

6. Flip the piece over, horizontally.

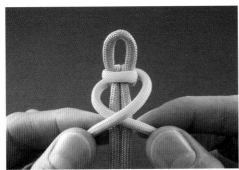

7. Cross the horizontal cords over the vertical cords, right over left.

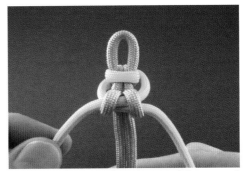

8. Circle the vertical cords around the crossed cords, between the legs above.

9. Adjust the cords until the piece is firm.

10. Flip the piece over, horizontally.

11. Cross the horizontal cords over the vertical cords, right over left.

12. Circle the vertical cords around the crossed cords, between the legs above.

13. Adjust the cords until the piece is firm.

14. Repeat Steps 6 through 13 until a minimum 5 in. (12.7 cm) of cord ends remain.

15. Tie a 4-Strand Diamond Knot (see Page 50) with the horizontal and vertical cords.

16. Carefully snip and singe the cord ends to complete the Sine Wave Sinnet Fob.

DIVIDED SINE WAVE SINNET

The Divided Sine Wave Sinnet draws extra attention to its wave pattern with the addition of the third cord. Slightly thicker than its namesake, the tie's construction is sturdier and more solid. It's also a great way to represent your favorite school or team colors.

Cord Used: *Three 5 ft. (1.5 m) Cords = 3.5 in. (8.9 cm) Key Fob*

Component Parts: *Sine Wave Sinnet + Integrated Contrasting Cords*

1. Start with bights created at the middle of two cords.

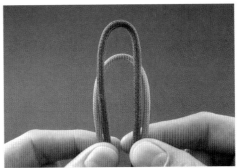

2. Drop one of the cords down 0.5 in. (1.3 cm) behind the bight of the other.

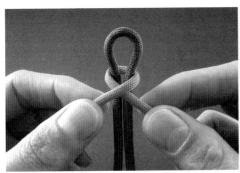

3. Cross the back cords over the front (vertical) cords, right over left.

4. Circle the vertical cords around the crossed cords, between the legs above.

5. Leaving a 0.5 in. (1.3 cm) bight on top, pull the right and left horizontal cords out.

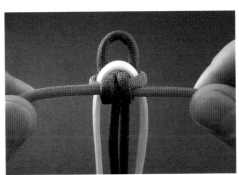

6. Lace the third cord over the vertical cords and through the loop of the horizontal cords. Stop at its middle.

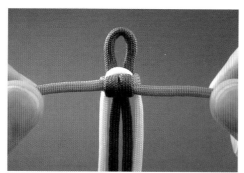

7. Tighten the right and left horizontal cords over the third cord.

8. Flip the piece over, horizontally.

9. Cross the horizontal cords over the vertical cords, right over left.

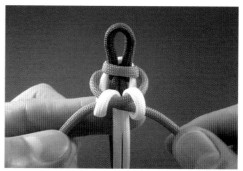

10. Circle the back-vertical cords around the crossed cords, between their legs above.

11. Adjust the cords until the piece is firm.

12. Flip the piece over, horizontally.

13. Cross the horizontal cords over the vertical cords, right over left.

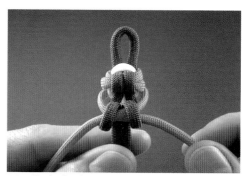

14. Circle the front-vertical cords around the crossed cords, between their legs above.

15. Adjust the cords until the piece is firm.

16. Repeat Steps 8 through 15 until a minimum 5 in. (12.7 cm) of cord ends remain.

17. Tie a 4-Strand Diamond Knot around the front vertical cords (see Page 50) with the horizontal and back-vertical cords.

18. Carefully snip and singe the cord ends to complete the Divided Sine Wave Sinnet Fob.

WIDE SINE WAVE SINNET

The Wide Sine Wave Sinnet takes the waveform that defines this tying genre in a lateral direction. Rather than utilizing the third cord to simply establish a color difference, the added cord generates a wider form with colors organized spectrally.

Cord Used: *Three 6 ft. (1.8 m) Cords = 3.5 in. (8.9 cm) Key Fob*

Component Parts: *Sine Wave Sinnet + Inside Tucks + Spectrally Clustered Cords*

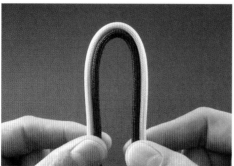

1. Start with bights created at the middle of two cords.

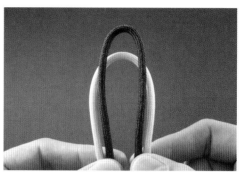

2. Drop one of the cords down 0.5 in. (1.3 cm) behind the bight of the other.

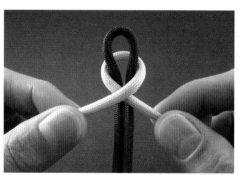

3. Cross the back cords over the front (vertical) cords, right over left.

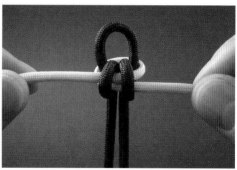

4. Circle the vertical cords around the crossed cords, between the legs above.

5. Leaving a 0.5 in. (1.3 cm) bight on top, pull the right and left horizontal cords out.

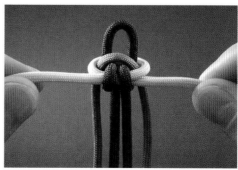

6. Lace the third cord over the vertical cords and through the loop of the horizontal cords. Stop at its middle.

7. Circle the right and left running ends of the third cord around the crossed cords…

8. …outside themselves and before the right and left crooks above.

9. Adjust the cords until the piece is firm.

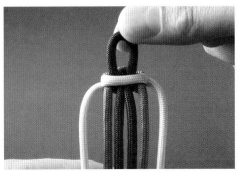

10. Flip the piece over, horizontally.

11. Cross the horizontal cords over the vertical cords, right over left.

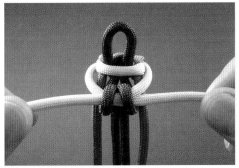

12. Circle the inner-vertical cords around the crossed cords, between the legs above.

13. Circle the right and left running ends of the outer-vertical cords around the crossed cords…

14. …outside themselves and before the right and left crooks above.

15. Adjust the cords until the piece is firm.

16. Flip the piece over, horizontally.

17. Cross the horizontal cords over the vertical cords, right over left.

18. Circle the inner-vertical cords around the crossed cords, between the legs above.

19. Circle the right and left running ends of the outer-vertical cords around the crossed cords…

20. …outside themselves and before the right and left crooks above.

21. Adjust the cords until the piece is firm.

22. Repeat Steps 10 through 21 until a minimum 5 in. (12.7 cm) of cord ends remain.

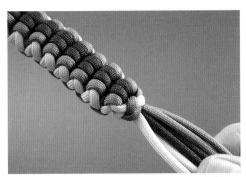

23. Tie a 4-Strand Diamond Knot around the inner-vertical cords (see Page 50) with the horizontal and outer-vertical cords.

24. Carefully snip and singe the cord ends to complete the Wide Sine Wave Sinnet Fob.

TEMPLE TOWER SINNET

The Temple Tower Sinnet is the tiered, radially symmetrical version of the Sine Wave Sinnet. Reminiscent of the towers within the Angkor Wat temple complex in Cambodia, the tie makes an unconventional-looking fob that has a good feel when gripped in the hand.

Cord Used: *One 8 ft. (2.4 m) Cord & Two 6 ft. (1.8 m) Cords = 3.5 in. (8.9 cm) Key Fob*

Component Parts: *Sine Wave Sinnet + Rotational Orientation + Contrasting Cords*

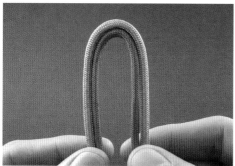

1.   Start with bights created at the middle of two cords, one short and one long.

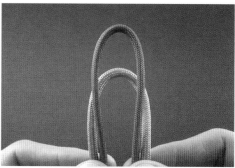

2.   Drop the short cord down 0.5 in. (1.3 cm), behind the bight of the long cord.

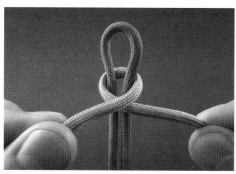

3.   Cross the back cords over the front (vertical) cords, right over left.

4.   Circle the vertical cords around the crossed cords, between the legs above.

5.   Leaving a 0.5 in. (1.3 cm) bight on top, pull the right and left horizontal cords out.

6.   Lace the second short cord over the vertical cords and through the loop of the horizontal cords. Stop at its middle.

7. Tighten the right and left horizontal cords over the second short cord.

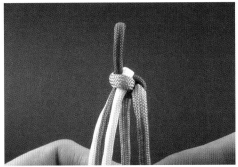

8. Rotate the left side of the piece 90° (toward you), horizontally.

9. Cross the right and left cords over the vertical cords, right over left.

10. Circle the vertical cords around the crossed cords, between the legs above.

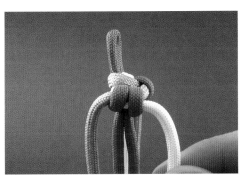

11. Adjust the cords until the piece is firm.

12. Rotate the left side of the piece 90° (toward you), horizontally.

13. Cross the right and left cords over the vertical cords, right over left.

14. Circle the vertical cords around the crossed cords, between the legs above.

15. Adjust the cords until the piece is firm.

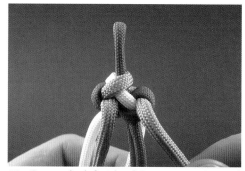

16. Rotate the left side of the piece 90° (toward you), horizontally.

17. Cross the right and left cords over the vertical cords, right over left.

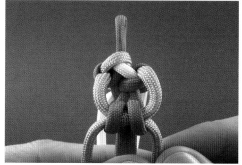

18. Circle the vertical cords around the crossed cords, between the legs above.

19. Adjust the cords until the piece is firm.

20. Rotate the left side of the piece 90° (toward you), horizontally.

21. Cross the right and left cords over the vertical cords, right over left.

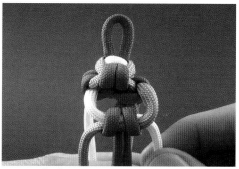

22. Circle the vertical cords around the crossed cords, between the legs above.

23. Adjust the cords until the piece is firm.

24. Repeat Steps 8 through 23 until a minimum 5 in. (12.7 cm) of cord ends remain.

25. Tie a 4-Strand Diamond Knot around the long vertical cords (see Page 50) with the short horizontal cords.

26. Carefully snip and singe the cord ends to complete the Temple Tower Sinnet Fob.

DESERT FLOWER MEDALLION

The Desert Flower Medallion is one of my favorite designs in this book. Producing a radiant flower pattern with a seamless necklace attached, its eye-catching appearance dazzles all who see it—a fact that makes this tie an awesome gift or item to sell.

Cord Used: *One 7 ft. (2.1 m) Cord & One 5 ft. (1.5 cm) Cord = 1.5 in. (3.8 cm) Medallion*

Component Parts: *Sine Wave Sinnet + Left-Left Single Cord Loops + Pulled Loop Lanyard*

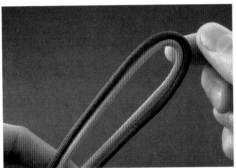

1. Start with bights created at the middle of the two cords.

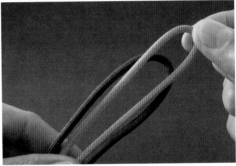

2. Drop the short cord down 0.5 in. (1.3 cm), behind the bight of the long cord.

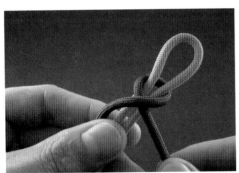

3. Cross the back cords over the front (vertical) cords, right over left.

4. Pull the bight above the crossed cords out 1 ft. (0.3 m).

5. At the point where the back cords cross, circle the left vertical cord…

6. …around the crossed cords, left of the legs above.

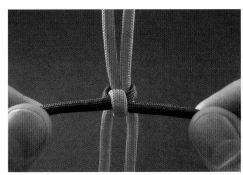

7. Tighten the piece until firm, leaving the 1 ft. (0.3 m) long bight on top.

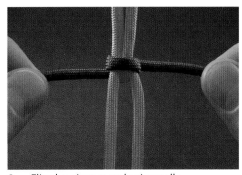

8. Flip the piece over, horizontally.

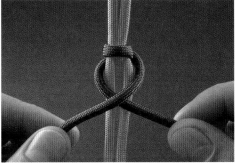

9. Cross the horizontal cords over the vertical cords, right over left. Then circle the left vertical cord…

10. …around the crossed cords, left of the legs above.

11. Adjust the cords until the piece is firm.

12. Repeat Steps 8 through 11 twelve more times, or until a total of fourteen "flower petals" have been made.

13. Flip the piece over, horizontally.

14. Arch the piece until its bottom left and right sides nearly touch.

15. Pull the lower right loop out…

16. …until a 0.5 in. (1.3 cm) loop remains at the bottom.

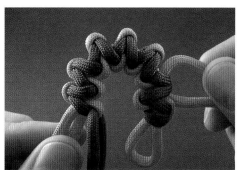

17. Take up the slack in the lower right loop by pulling the loop above it out.

18. Continue taking up slack in each loop above the one below…

19. …until all slack, above the bottom loop, is pulled out the (middlemost) top loop.

20. Rotate the piece counterclockwise 90°.

21. Now, take the tip of the front vertical (long) cord in hand…

22. …and insert it through the loop above.

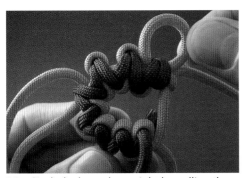

23. Cinch the loop above tight by pulling the loop above it out.

24. Pull the front vertical cord through the cinched bottom loop until both sides of the piece circle up.

25. Repeat Steps 17 through 19.

26. Tie a 4-Strand Diamond Knot (see Page 50) with the horizontal and vertical cords.

27. Carefully snip and singe the cord ends.

28. The completed Desert Flower Medallion Necklace.

Chapter 5

Den of Snakes

SNAKE KNOT

The Snake Knot is a popular Chinese knot, reputed to impart good luck to those who make or receive it as a gift. The tie is also seen adorning the ends of prayer beads used by Hindus and Buddhists who believe it has spiritual significance.

Cord Used: *One 7 ft. (2.1 m) Cord = 7.5 in. (19.1 cm) Bracelet*

Component Parts: *Historical Knot*

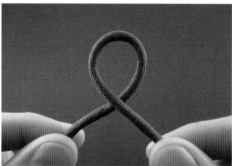

1. At the middle of the cord, make a counterclockwise loop.

2. Bight the right running end through the loop…

3. …and tighten, leaving a 0.5 in. (1.3 cm) loop in the Slip Knot made.

4. Hook the right running end left, over the left cord.

5. Then hook it right, around the back of the left cord, making a counterclockwise loop.

6. Hook the circled cord right, under the leg of the looped cord.

7. Then hook it left, over the front of the looped cord and through its counter-clockwise loop.

8. Adjust the cords until the knot is firm.

9. Repeat Steps 4 through 8 until a minimum 5 in. (12.7 cm) of cord ends remain.

10. Tie a 2-Strand Diamond Knot (see Page 4) with the vertical cords.

11. Carefully snip and singe the Diamond Knot ends.

12. The completed Snake Knot Bracelet.

Mystic Snake Knot

The Mystic Snake Knot demonstrates what mixing and matching fusion knotting techniques can produce. Generating a bead like pattern along an otherwise single-color Snake Knot, the array can be dotted, dashed, or varied.

Cord Used: *One 8 ft. (2.4 m) Cord & One 6 ft. (1.8 cm) Cord = 7.5 in. (19.1 cm) Bracelet*

Component Parts: *Snake Knots + Mystical Tunneling Technique + Contrasting Cords*

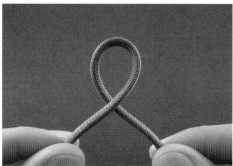

1. At the middle of the short cord, make a clockwise loop.

2. Then cross the middle of the long cord across the apex of the right running end.

3. Bight the right running end over the second cord and through the loop.

4. Tighten the piece, leaving a 0.5 in. (1.3 cm) loop in the Slip Knot made.

5. Lift the ends of the long cord until they extend beyond the ends of the short cord.

6. Hook the right running end left, over all three vertical cords.

7. Then hook it right, around the back of the vertical cords, making a counterclockwise loop.

8. Hook the leftmost circled cord right, under the vertical cords, and the leg of the looped cord.

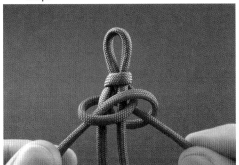

9. Then hook it left, over the front of the looped cord and through its counter-clockwise loop.

10. Adjust the cords until the knot is firm.

11. Repeat Steps 6 through 10 four more times.

12. Lift the short cord ends until they extend beyond the long cord ends.

13. Repeat Steps 6 through 10 two times.

14. Lift the long cord ends until they extend beyond the short cord ends.

15. Repeat Steps 6 through 10 five times.

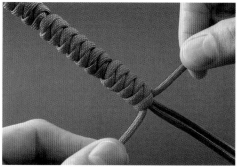

16. Repeat Steps 12 through 15 until a minimum 5 in. (12.7 cm) of cord ends remain.

17. Tighten the last knot firmly, then carefully snip and singe its ends.

18. Tie a 2-Strand Diamond Knot (see Page 4) with the remaining vertical cords.

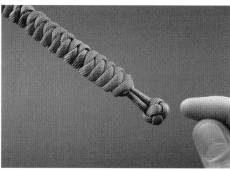

19. Carefully snip and singe the Diamond Knot ends.

20. The completed Mystic Snake Knot Bracelet.

MATED SNAKE KNOTS

Mated Snake Knots are two side-by-side interlocked snake knots. The technique shown can be expanded to generate a threesome or even a foursome of "mated" knots, making an ever wider bracelet, belt, or strap.

Cord Used: *Two 8 ft. (2.4 m) Cords = 7.5 in. (19.1 cm) Bracelet*

Component Parts: *Snake Knots + Interlocking Cords + Integrated Contrasting Cords*

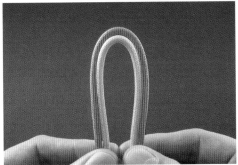

1. Start with bights created at the middle of the two cords.

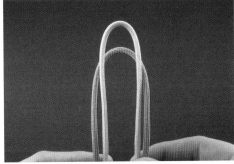

2. Drop one of the cords down 0.5 in. (1.3 cm), behind the bight of the other.

3. Cross the back cords over the front (vertical) cords, right over left.

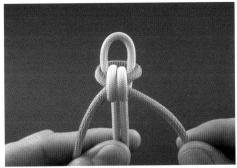

4. Circle the vertical cords around the crossed cords, between the legs above.

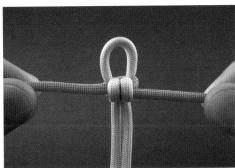

5. Tighten the piece until firm, leaving a 0.5 in. (1.3 cm) bight on top.

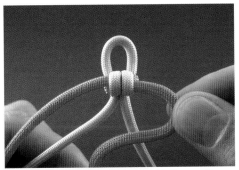

6. Hook the right running end left, over its nearest vertical cord.

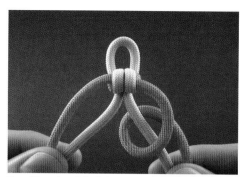

7. Then hook it right, around the back of the vertical cord, making a counterclockwise loop.

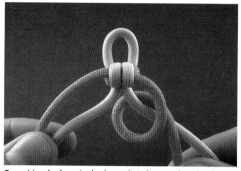

8. Hook the circled cord right, under the leg of the looped cord.

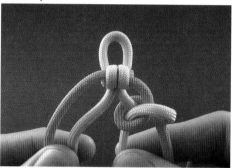

9. Then hook it left, over the front of the looped cord and through its counter-clockwise loop.

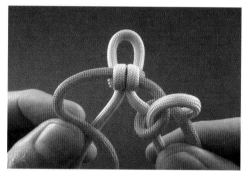

10. Hook the left running end right, over its nearest vertical cord.

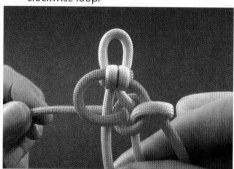

11. Then hook it left, through the crook of the counterclockwise loop…

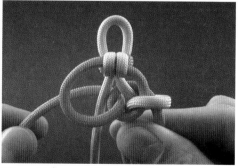

12. …and around the back of the vertical cord, making a clockwise loop.

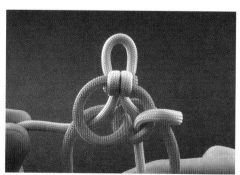

13. Hook the circled cord left, under the leg of the looped cord.

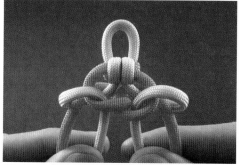

14. Then hook it right, over the front of the looped cord and through its clockwise loop.

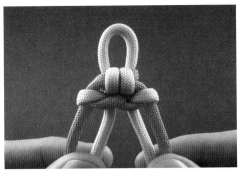

15. Adjust the cords until the knots are firm.

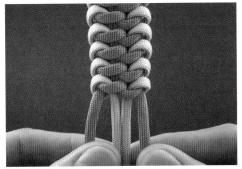

16. Repeat Steps 6 through 15 until a minimum 5 in. (12.7 cm) of cord ends remain.

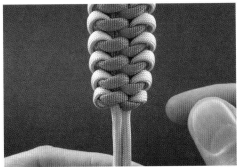

17. Tighten the last knots firmly, then carefully snip and singe their ends.

18. Tie a 2-Strand Diamond Knot (see Page 4) with the remaining vertical cords.

19. Carefully snip and singe the Diamond Knot ends.

20. The completed Mated Snake Knots Bracelet.

SNAKES CLIMBING CHAINED ENDLESS FALLS

Snake Knots and Endless Falls are the most adaptable ties that I know. How better to symbolize this fact than to bring these two tying genres together with Snakes Climbing Chained Endless Falls, a sturdy, strap-like tie that looks like no other.

Cord Used: *Three 8 ft. (2.4 m) Cords = 7.5 in. (19.1 cm) Bracelet*

Component Parts: *Snake Knots + Chained Endless Falls + Crossed Cords + Integrated Contrasting Cords*

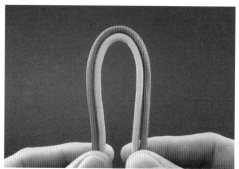

1. Start with bights created at the middle of two cords.

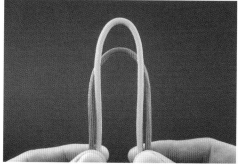

2. Drop one of the cords down 0.5 in. (1.3 cm), behind the bight of the other.

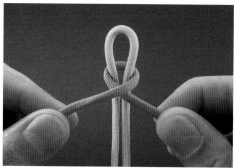

3. Cross the back cords over the front (vertical) cords, right over left.

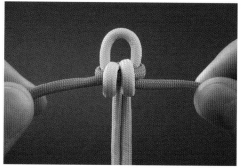

4. Circle the vertical cords around the crossed cords, between the legs above.

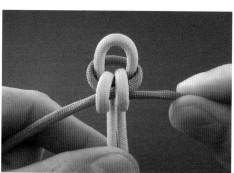

5. Leaving a 0.5 in. (1.3 cm) bight on top, pull the right and left horizontal cords out.

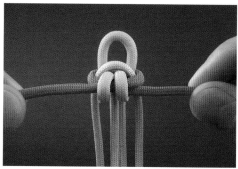

6. Lace the third cord over the vertical cords and through the loop of the horizontal cords. Stop at its middle.

7. Tighten the right and left horizontal cords over the third cord.

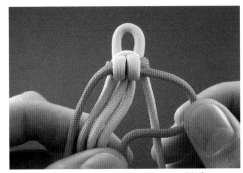

8. Hook the rightmost running end left, over its nearest vertical cord.

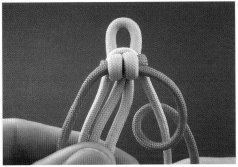

9. Then hook it right, around the back of the vertical cord, making a counterclockwise loop.

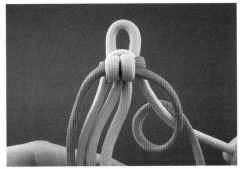

10. Hook the circled cord right, under the leg of the looped cord.

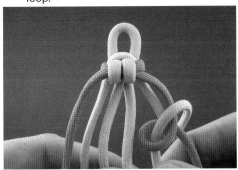

11. Then hook it left, over the front of the looped cord and through its counter-clockwise loop.

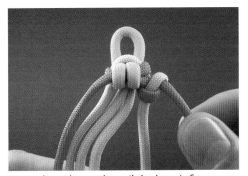

12. Adjust the cords until the knot is firm.

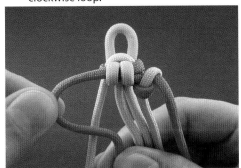

13. Hook the leftmost running end right, over its nearest vertical cord.

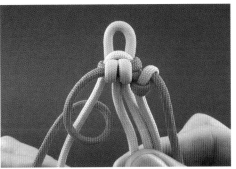

14. Then hook it left, around the back of the vertical cord, making a clockwise loop.

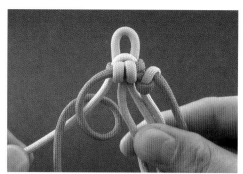

15. Hook the circled cord left, under the leg of the looped cord.

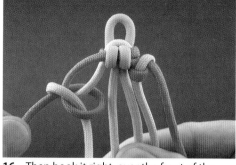

16. Then hook it right, over the front of the looped cord and through its clockwise loop.

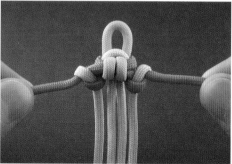

17. Adjust the cords until the knot is firm.

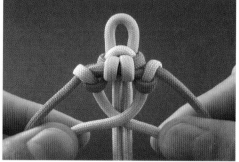

18. Cross the cords on either side of the middlemost vertical cords, right over left.

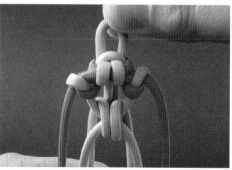

19. Circle the middlemost vertical cords around the crossed cords, outside the legs above.

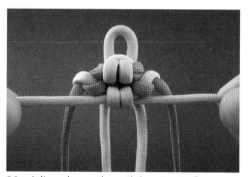

20. Adjust the cords until the piece is firm.

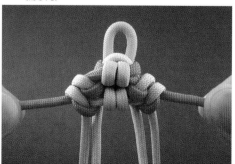

21. Repeat Steps 8 through 17.

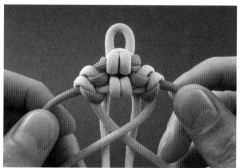

22. Cross the cords on either side of the middlemost vertical cords, right over left.

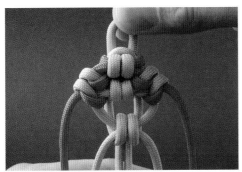

23. Circle the middlemost vertical cords around the crossed cords, between the legs above.

24. Adjust the cords until the piece is firm.

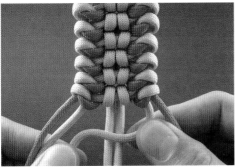

25. Repeat Steps 8 through 17.

26. Repeat Steps 18 through 25 until a minimum 5 in. (12.7 cm) of cord ends remain.

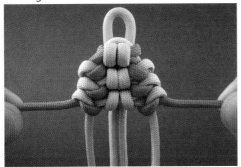

27. Hook the cord right of the middlemost vertical cords left, over the vertical cords.

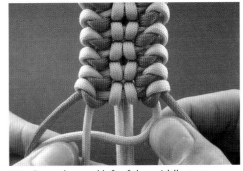

28. Drop the cord left of the middlemost vertical cords over the cord beneath it.

29. Then hook it right, under the vertical cords, and through the back of the right crook. Tighten firmly.

30. Hook the cord left of the middlemost vertical cords right, over the vertical cords.

31. Drop the cord right of the middlemost vertical cords over the cord beneath it.

32. Then hook it left, under the vertical cords, and through the back of the left crook. Tighten firmly.

33. Carefully snip and singe all knot ends. **Note:** Do not snip and singe the middlemost vertical cord ends.

34. Tie a 2-Strand Diamond Knot (see Page 4) with the remaining vertical cords.

35. Carefully snip and singe the Diamond Knot ends.

36. The completed Snakes Climbing Chained Endless Falls Bracelet.

TIKI BAR

The menacing grimace of a Tiki statue or wooden mask has become symbolic of various Polynesian cultures. In its knotted form, the Tiki Bar calls to these tropical cultures and the drinking establishments (i.e., "bars") that celebrate their aesthetic.

Cord Used: *Two 7 ft. (2.1 m) Cords = 7.5 in. (19.1 cm) Bracelet*

Component Parts: *Alternating Snake Knots + Crossed Cords + Integrated Contrasting Cords*

1. Start with bights created at the middle of the two cords.

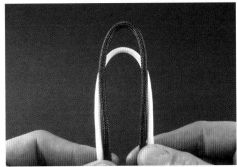

2. Drop one of the cords down 0.5 in. (1.3 cm), behind the bight of the other.

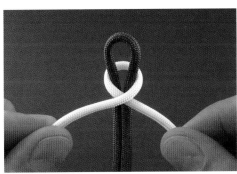

3. Cross the back cords over the front (vertical) cords, right over left.

4. Circle the vertical cords around the crossed cords, between the legs above.

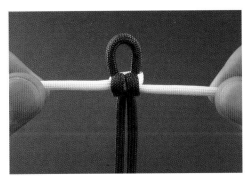

5. Tighten the piece until firm, leaving a 0.5 in. (1.3 cm) bight on top.

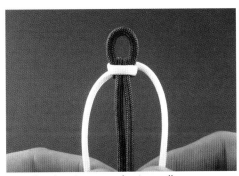

6. Flip the piece over, horizontally.

7. Hook the right middlemost vertical cord right, over the cord next to it.

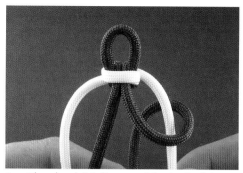

8. Then hook it left, around the back of the cord, making a clockwise loop.

9. Hook the circled cord left, under the leg of the looped cord.

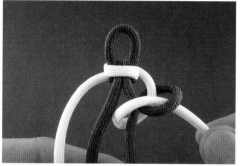

10. Then hook it right, over the front of the looped cord and through its clockwise loop.

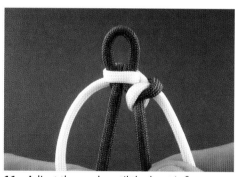

11. Adjust the cords until the knot is firm.

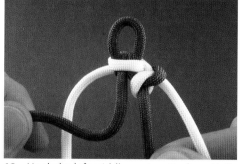

12. Hook the left middlemost vertical cord left, over the cord next to it.

13. Then hook it right, around the back of the cord, making a counterclockwise loop.

14. Hook the circled cord right, under the leg of the looped cord.

15. Then hook it left, over the front of the looped cord and through its counter-clockwise loop.

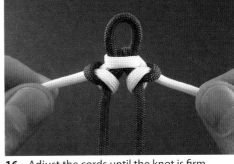

16. Adjust the cords until the knot is firm.

17. Cross the middlemost vertical cords, right over left.

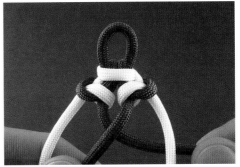

18. Hook the right middlemost cord right, under the cord next to it.

19. Then hook it left, over the front of the cord, making a counterclockwise loop.

20. Hook the circled cord left, over the leg of the looped cord.

21. Then hook it right, around the back of the looped cord and through its counter-clockwise loop.

22. Adjust the cords until the knot is firm.

23. Hook the left middlemost cord left, under the cord next to it.

24. Then hook it right, over the front of the cord, making a clockwise loop.

25. Hook the circled cord right, over the leg of the looped cord.

26. Then hook it left, around the back of the looped cord and through its clockwise loop.

27. Adjust the cords until the knot is firm.

28. Repeat Steps 7 through 27 until a minimum 10 in. (25.4 cm) of cord ends remain.

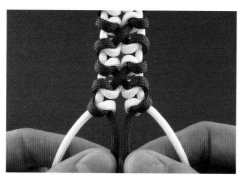

29. Then repeat Steps 7 through 16.

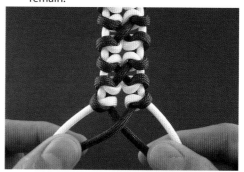

30. Cross the middlemost vertical cords, right over left.

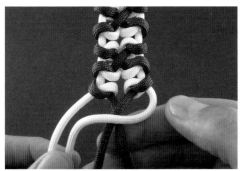

31. Hook the rightmost cord left, over the middlemost vertical cords.

32. Drop the leftmost cord over the cord beneath it.

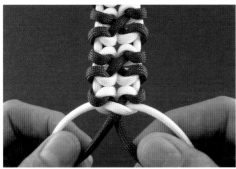

33. Then hook it right, under the vertical cords, and through the back of the right crook. Tighten firmly.

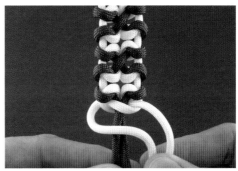

34. Hook the leftmost cord right, over the middlemost vertical cords.

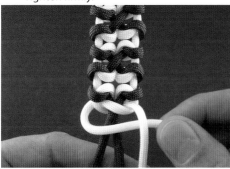

35. Drop the rightmost cord over the cord beneath it.

36. Then hook it left, under the vertical cords, and through the back of the left crook. Tighten firmly.

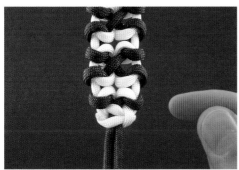

37. Carefully snip and singe the horizontal cord ends, at their base.

38. Tie a 2-Strand Diamond Knot (see Page 4) with the vertical cords.

39. Carefully snip and singe the Diamond Knot ends.

40. The completed Tiki Bar Bracelet.

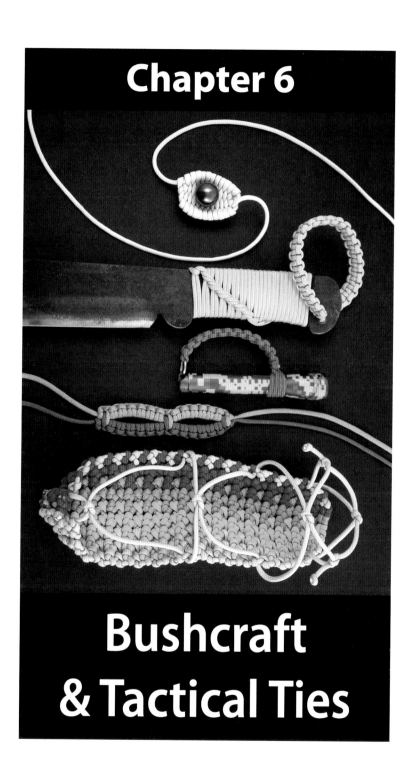

Chapter 6

Bushcraft & Tactical Ties

SINGLE-CORD ROCK SLING

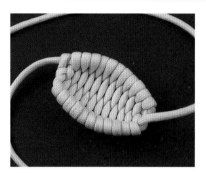

The Single-Cord Rock Sling is my favorite improvised weapon. Once the tying technique is mastered, a completed piece can be made in minutes. In the hands of a seasoned slinger, the tie can be used to protect oneself or effectively target prey.

Cord Used: *One 14 ft. (4.3 m) Cord = 2 ft. (0.6 m) Lines Leading to a 3 in. (7.6 cm) Long by 2 in. (5.1 cm) Wide Pouch*

Component Parts: *Overhand Loop + Woven Bights + Barrel Knot*

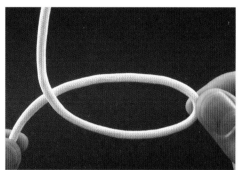

1. Four ft. (1.2 m) right of the left cord end, make a 3 in. (7.6 cm) long clockwise loop.

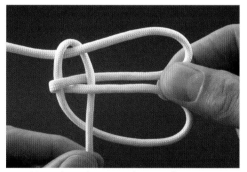

2. Hook the left cord end right, around the ascending cord, and above the loop.

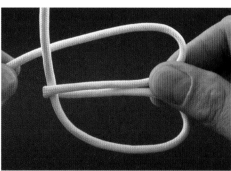

3. Bight the cord end back on itself at 3 in. (7.6 cm), passing it under the ascending cord.

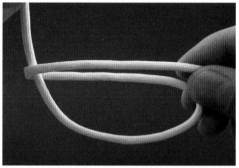

4. Now, drop the ascending cord, weaving it under, over, under, and over the cords beneath it.

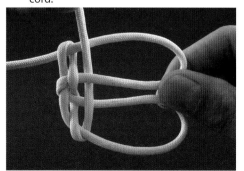

5. Bight the cord back on itself, weaving it under, over, under, and over the cords above it.

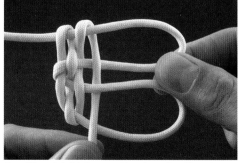

6. Then bight the cord back on itself again, weaving it under, over, under, and over the cords beneath it.

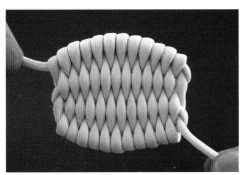

7. Repeat Steps 4 through 6 until a 3 in. (7.6 cm) long pouch is made.

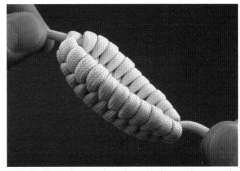

8. Pull on the cord ends and shape the pouch until it's slightly concave.

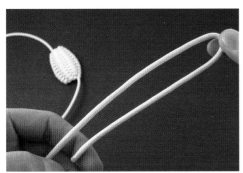

9. Two and a half ft. (0.76 m) from the pouch make a bight.

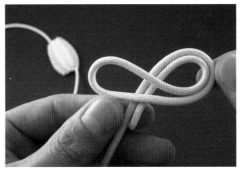

10. Hook the bight clockwise, making a double corded loop with its standing ends.

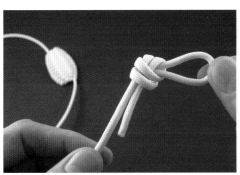

11. Insert the bight through the loop, making sure its tip is 2 ft. (0.61 m) from the end of the pouch.

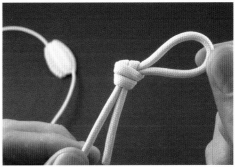

12. Tighten the Overhand Loop made, firmly, making sure it fits comfortably…

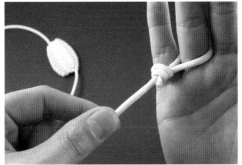

13. …around your ring finger. Then carefully snip and singe the short end below it.

14. Two ft. (0.61 m) from the other end of the pouch, draw the cord across your forefinger.

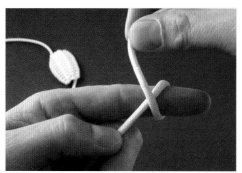

15. Circle the cord around your forefinger, and over itself, once…

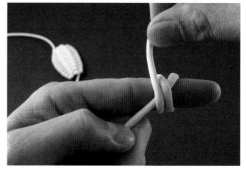

16. …twice…

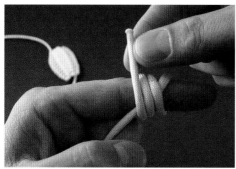

17. …and then a third time.

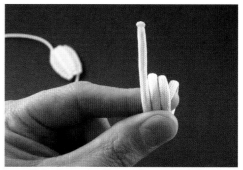

18. Slide the coils off your finger, while holding them in place.

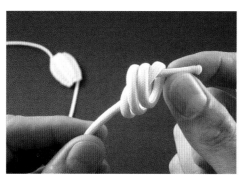

19. Then insert the running end through the middle of the coils.

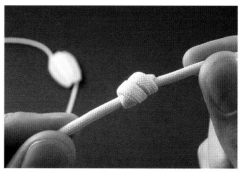

20. Gently pull on the running end until the Barrel Knot made is tightened firmly at 2 ft. (0.61 m)

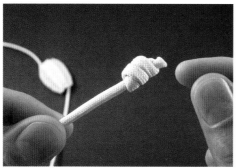

21. Carefully snip and singe the knot end.

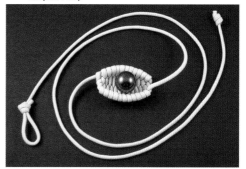

22. The completed Single-Cord Rock Sling. For use, search "How to Use a Rock Sling" on YouTube.com.

TACTICAL FLASHLIGHT STRAP

The Tactical Flashlight Strap combines an emergency source of paracord with the mechanical versatility of a tactical strap. Light your way while maintaining your ability to carry a second item, accomplish delicate tasks, or quickly throw a fistloaded punch.

Cord Used: *One 6 ft. (1.8 m) Cord = 5 in. (12.7 cm) Tactical Strap*

Component Parts: *Mini Maglite® + ¾ In. (1.9 cm) Dia. Split Ring + Strangle Knot (Modified) + Solomon Bar*

1. Obtain a Mini Maglite® or a flashlight of a similar design…

2. …and connect a ¾ in. (1.9 cm) diameter split ring to its tail.

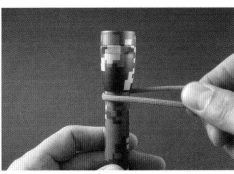

3. Hook the middle of the cord around the back of the flashlight's neck, below its head.

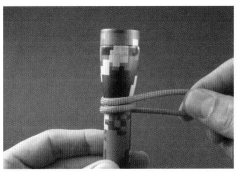

4. Circle the left cord end right, around the neck, once…

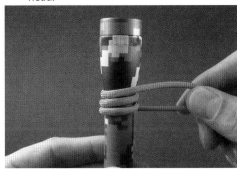

5. …twice…

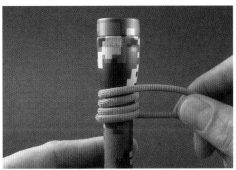

6. …and then a third time.

7. Then take the tip of the lower cord end in hand…

8. …and insert it under the coils above.

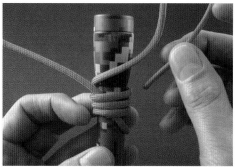

9. Then take the upper cord end in hand…

10. …and insert it under the coils below, running it parallel to and alongside the other cord end.

11. Pull on the lower and upper cord ends until the Strangle Knot made is tightened firmly.

12. Flip the flashlight over, upside down. Then draw both cord ends…

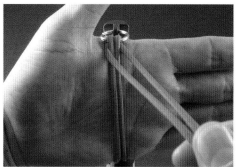

13. …comfortably over the palm of your hand and through the split ring, as shown.

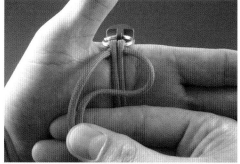

14. Hook the right running end left, over the vertical cords.

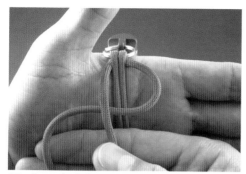

15. Drop the left running end over the cord beneath it.

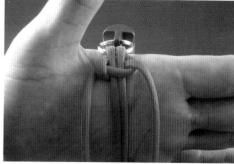

16. Then hook it right, under the vertical cords, and through the back of the right crook. Tighten firmly.

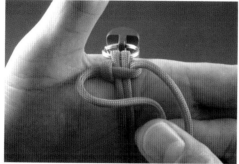

17. Hook the left running end right, over the vertical cords.

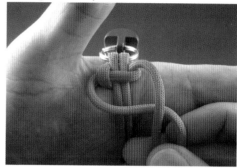

18. Drop the right running end over the cord beneath it.

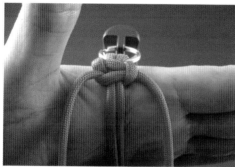

19. Then hook it left, under the vertical cords, and through the back of the left crook. Tighten firmly.

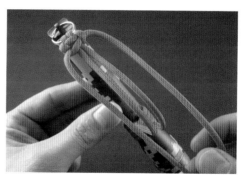

20. Slide the piece off your hand.

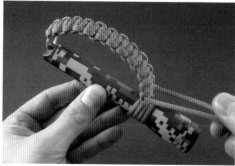

21. Repeat Steps 14 through 19 until the top of the Strangle Knot is reached.

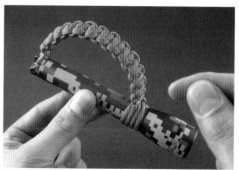

22. Carefully snip and singe the horizontal cord ends.

23. The completed Tactical Flashlight Strap.

24. With the strap in place, you can use your hand to carry a second item.

25. Or you can walk with your hand relaxed at your side, to illuminate the space before you…

26. …ready to use the flashlight as a fistload to increase the force of your punch.

NO-SLIP MACHETE GRIP

The No-Slip Machete Grip is a slip resistant handle wrap coupled with a strap that provides leverage and stability. Together these two elements reduce the chances of a machete being pulled from the hand, while chopping or swinging.

Cord Used: *One 24 ft. (7.3 m) Cord = 5 in. (12.7 cm) Handle Wrap & 10 in. (25.4 cm) Strap*

Component Parts: *Jungle Master® Rambo Machete + French Whipping + Solomon Bar*

1. Obtain a Jungle Master® Rambo Machete or a machete of a similar design…

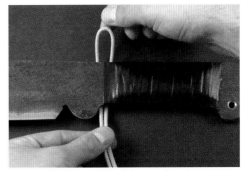

2. Bight the middle of the cord under the bolster of the machete.

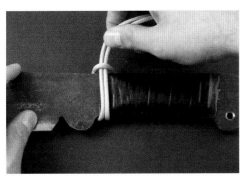

3. Draw both cord ends over the bolster and through the bight above, making a Cow Hitch.

4. Adjust the hitch until it's tightened firmly around the bolster.

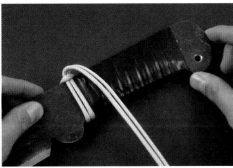

5. Tilt the handle of the machete 45° left.

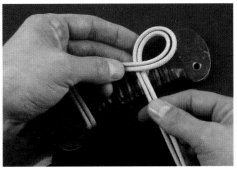

6. Make a clockwise loop with the cord ends.

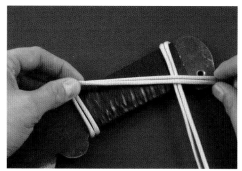

7. Carefully slide the loop around the pommel…

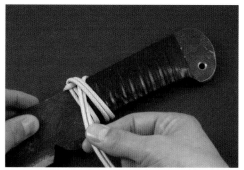

8. …and then down the handle of the machete, making a Half Hitch above the hitch below.

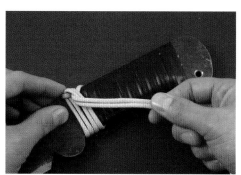

9. Adjust the Half Hitch until it's tightened firmly around the handle.

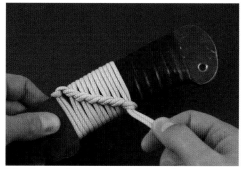

10. Repeat Steps 6 through 9 until you reach the inner edge of the handle. Then…

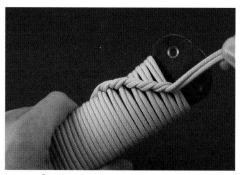

11. …flip the machete over, vertically. Continue repeating Steps 6 through 9 until you reach the pommel.

12. To fix the series of Half Hitches (i.e., French Whipping) in place, lift the standing ends of the last hitch…

13. …tuck the running ends underneath the lifted ends…

14. …and then insert the running ends through the loop made. Tighten firmly.

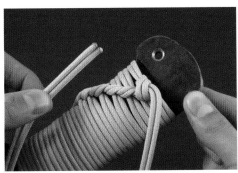

15. Now take the tips of the running ends in hand…

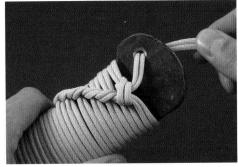

16. …and insert them through the pommel hole.

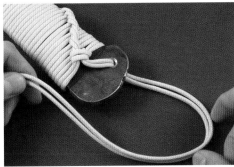

17. Draw the running ends out 10 in. (25.4 cm).

18. Then hook the running ends, in opposing directions, through the cords above the pommel hole.

19. Hook the right running end left, over the vertical cords.

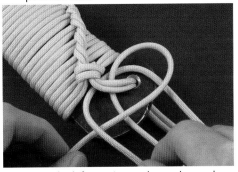

20. Drop the left running end over the cord beneath it.

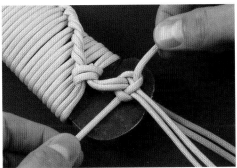

21. Then hook it right, under the vertical cord, and through the back of the right crook. Tighten firmly.

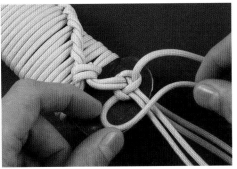

22. Hook the left running end right, over the vertical cords.

23. Drop the right running end over the cord beneath it.

24. Then hook it left, under the vertical cords, and through the back of the left crook. Tighten firmly.

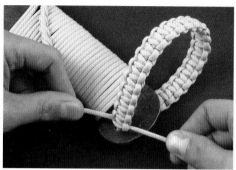

25. Repeat Steps 19 through 24 until the opposite side of the pommel is reached.

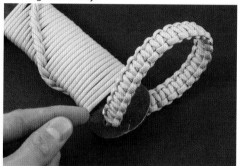

26. Carefully snip and singe the horizontal cord ends, at their base.

27. The completed No-Slip Machete Grip—handle revealed.

28. The completed No-Slip Machete Grip—ready for use!

EMERGENCY SNOW GOGGLES

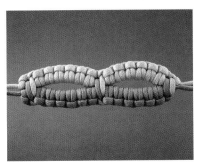

Emergency Snow Goggles are modeled after the traditional snow goggles used by the Inuit people of the Arctic. Snow blindness, a painful eye condition caused by overexposure to UV light, can be prevented or mitigated with knowledge of this paracord design.

Cord Used: *Two 7.5 ft. (2.3 m) Cords = 5 in. (12.7 cm) Goggles*

Component Parts: *Paired Slip Knot Loops + Paired Cow Hitches + Opposing Half Hitches*

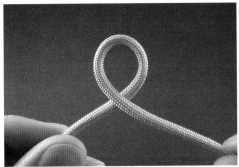

1. Approximately 2 ft. (0.61 m) left of the right cord end, make a counterclockwise loop.

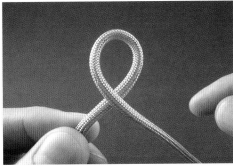

2. Maintain the short cord end on the right.

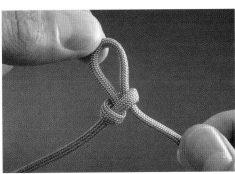

3. Bight the right cord end through the loop, making a Slip Knot.

4. Pull the loop of the Slip Knot out 6 in. (15.2 cm) and tighten.

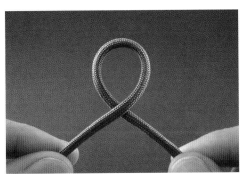

5. Approximately 2 ft. (0.61 m) right of the left cord end, make a clockwise loop.

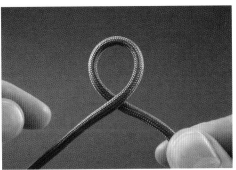

6. Maintain the short cord end on the left.

7. Bight the left cord end through the loop, making a Slip Knot.

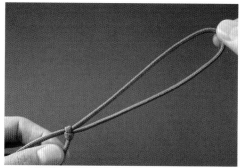

8. Pull the loop of the Slip Knot out 6 in. (15.2 cm) and tighten.

9. Line up the slip knots side-by-side with the short ends facing each another.

10. Hook the right running end left, over and around both vertical loops.

11. Then insert the running end through the back of the right crook. Tighten firmly.

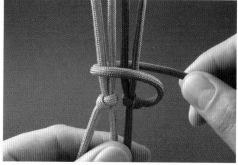

12. Hook the left running end right, over and around both vertical loops.

13. Then insert the running end through the back of the left crook. Tighten firmly.

14. Hook the right running end left, over and around the right vertical loop.

15. Then insert the running end through the back of the right crook. Tighten firmly.

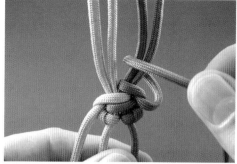

16. Hook the right running end left, under and around the right vertical loop.

17. Then insert the running end through the front of the right crook. Tighten firmly.

18. Repeat Steps 14 through 17 five more times.

19. Repeat Steps 14 through 18 around the left vertical loop, in reflection of the right vertical loop.

20. Then repeat Steps 10 through 13.

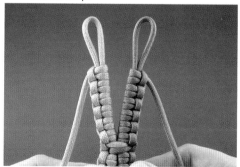

21. Repeat Steps 14 through 19…

22. …and Steps 10 through 13, again.

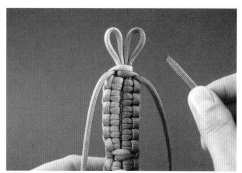

23. Now take the tip of the right running end in hand…

24. …and insert it through the right vertical loop.

25. Take the tip of the left running end in hand…

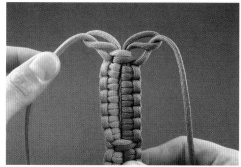

26. …and insert it through the left vertical loop.

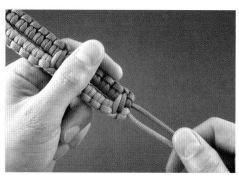

27. To firm up the piece, take hold of the standing ends…

28. …and pull firmly. This will cinch the right and left vertical loops around the running ends.

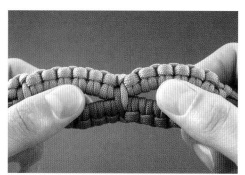

29. Adjust the piece until the eye slits are just narrow enough to see through.

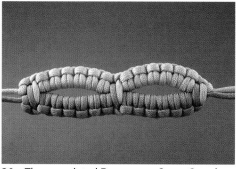

30. The completed Emergency Snow Goggles.

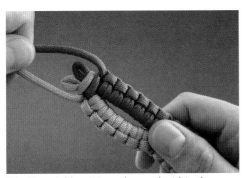

31. To quickly retrieve the cord within the goggles, slide the running ends out of the loops…

32. …and then pull on the standing ends.

33. As you continue to pull, the piece will turn from goggles…

34. …to a bundle of unknotted cords in less than 5 seconds!

BUSH SANDALS

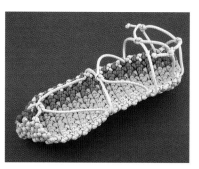

Bush Sandals are a reliable means of achieving emergency foot protection. Great for situations when your shoes are lost in mud, ditched while swimming, or you had to bug out before grabbing them. The sandals shield the soles from cuts and abrasions, and provide traction on slippery surfaces.

Cord Used: *Five 20 ft. (6.1 m) Cords = 12 in. (30.5 cm) Long by 4.5 in. (11.4 cm) Wide Sandals*

Component Parts: *Cow Hitches + Locking Slip Knots + Square Knots + Webbed Lacing*

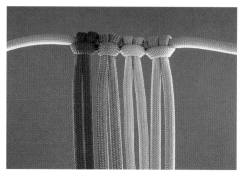

1. Begin by tying four Cow Hitches side-by-side around the middle of the fifth cord.

2. Flip the piece over, upside down.

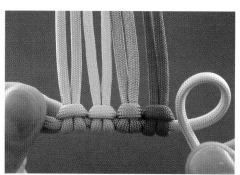

3. Make a counterclockwise loop with the rightmost cord end.

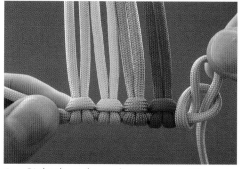

4. Bight the right cord's running end through the loop, making a Slip Knot.

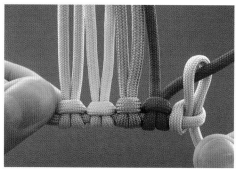

5. Insert the vertical cord to the left through the loop of the Slip Knot.

6. Then tighten the Slip Knot firmly around the vertical cord.

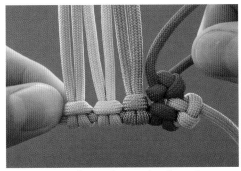

7. Continue forward repeating Steps 3 through 6…

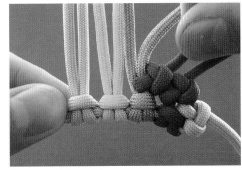

8. …making a Slip Knot…

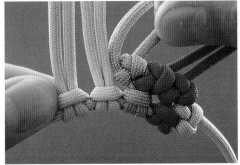

9. …with each vertical cord…

10. …that tightens firmly…

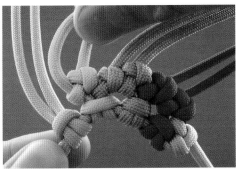

11. …around the cord to its left…

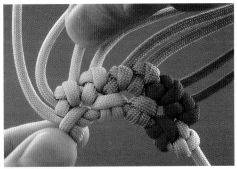

12. …until…

13. …the leftmost vertical cord becomes a Slip Knot…

14. …that tightens firmly around the leftmost cord end.

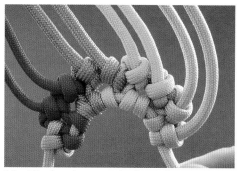

15. Flip the piece over, horizontally.

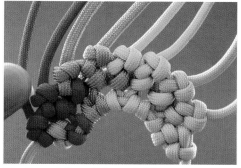

16. Repeat Steps 3 through 14.

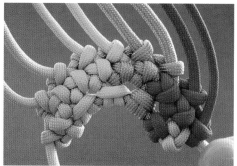

17. Flip the piece over, horizontally.

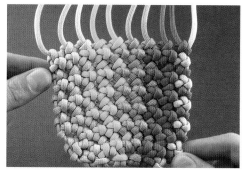

18. Then continue forward repeating Steps 3 through 17…

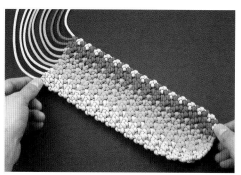

19. …until the sole of your sandal is 1 in. (2.5 cm) longer than the length of your foot.

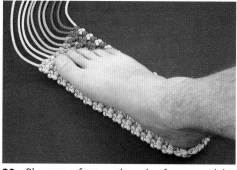

20. Place your foot on the sole of your sandal.

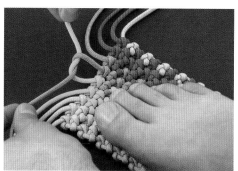

21. Take the middlemost vertical cords in hand and tie an Overhand Knot, right cord over left.

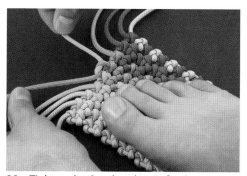

22. Tighten the Overhand Knot firmly.

23. Tie a second Overhand Knot, atop the first, left cord over right.

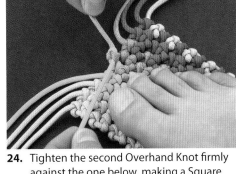

24. Tighten the second Overhand Knot firmly against the one below, making a Square Knot.

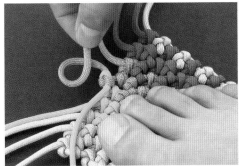

25. To lock the Square Knot in place…

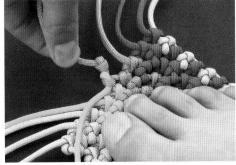

26. …tie single-cord Overhand Knots…

27. …in the knot ends.

28. Then carefully snip and singe the knot ends, above the single-cord Overhand Knots.

29. Repeat Steps 21 through 28…

30. …with the opposing vertical cords…

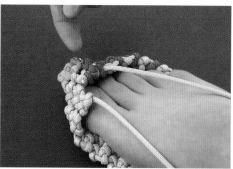

31. …left and right of the middlemost cords, until you reach the outermost cords.

32. Then tie a Square Knot 1 in. (2.5 cm) from the last (locked) Square Knot made.

33. Now, lace the left running end through the point in the sole at the top of your foot's inner arch.

34. Lace the right running end through the point in the sole at the top of your foot's outer arch.

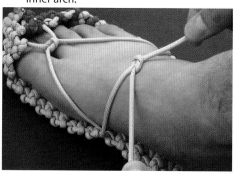

35. Tie a Square Knot atop the foot between the two points.

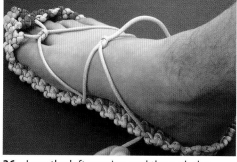

36. Lace the left running end through the point in the sole at the middle of your foot's inner arch.

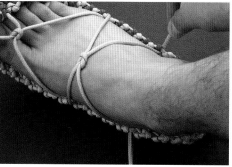

37. Lace the right running end through the point in the sole at the middle of your foot's outer arch.

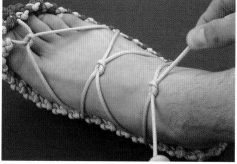

38. Tie a Square Knot atop the foot between the two points.

39. Lace the left running end through the point in the sole left of your foot's heel.

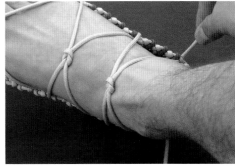

40. Lace the right running end through the point in the sole right of your foot's heel.

41. Tie a Square Knot 2 in. (5.1 cm) above the heel of your foot.

42. Take the left running end and tuck it under the diagonal cord in front of it.

43. Loop the running end around the cord and under itself.

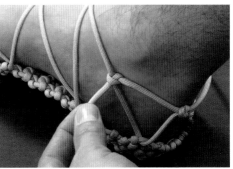

44. Insert the running end through the loop. Tighten the Overhand Knot made, firmly.

45. Bight the running end back on itself and under the diagonal cord behind it.

46 Insert the running end through the bight. Tighten the locked bight made, firmly.

47. Tie a single cord Overhand Knot 1 in. (2.5 cm) from the diagonal cord, then carefully snip and singe its end.

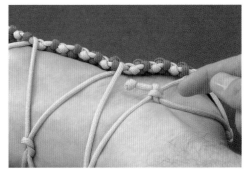

48. Repeat Steps 42 through 47 with the right running end, in reflection of the left running end.

49. The completed Bush Sandal. Make a second sandal (the same way as the first)…

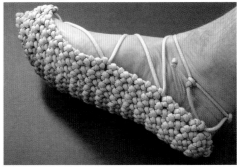

50. …and you'll be able to walk, run, jump, or climb knowing your feet are solidly protected!

Chapter 7

Pouches, Baskets, & Secret Spaces

SECRET COMPARTMENT FOB (ORIGINAL)

The (original) Secret Compartment Fob is a 6-Strand Crown Sinnet tied with a spiral weaving technique. The addition of the spiral weave generates a hollow elongated center that can hold a ferro rod, a rolled-up message, money, or any other object you can fit inside the tie.

Cord Used: *Three 5 ft. (1.5 m) Cords = 3.5 in. (8.9 cm) Key Fob*

Component Parts: *6-Strand Crown Sinnet + Spiral Weave*

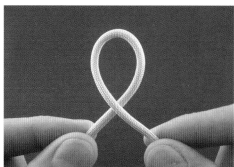

1. At the middle of the first cord, make a counterclockwise loop.

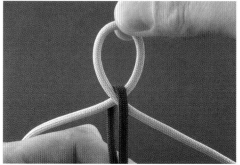

2. Lace the second cord through the loop, until its middle is reached.

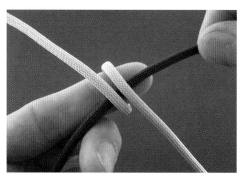

3. Flip the piece over, vertically, slide your forefinger into the loop, and extend the second cord laterally.

4. Arch the second cord ends over the first, in opposite directions, right cord above left.

5. Weave the lower cord end over the arch above it…

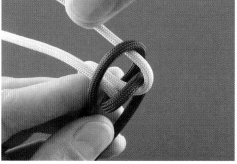

6. …and through the crook of the second arch.

7. Weave the upper cord end over the arch below it…

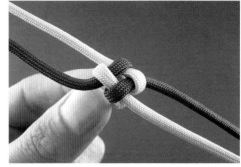

8. …and through the crook of the second arch, making a Crown Knot.

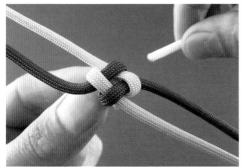

9. Take the tip of the third cord in hand…

10. …and insert it through the side of the Crown Knot. Tighten the knot firmly around the third cord.

11. Moving clockwise, cross the top cord over the upper right cord.

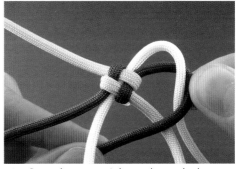

12. Cross the upper right cord over the lower right cord below it.

13. Cross the lower right cord over the bottom cord.

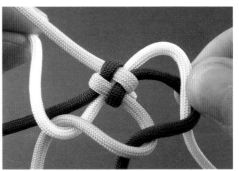

14. Cross the bottom cord over the lower left cord above it.

15. Cross the lower left cord over the upper left cord above it.

16. Then insert the upper left cord end over and through the top crook.

17. Adjust the cords until the knot is firm.

18. Repeat Steps 11 through 17 until a minimum 5 in. (12.7 cm) of cord ends remain.

19. **Note:** The center of the Secret Compartment Fob should be open and hollow.

20. If it is not, use a pencil to widen the center, top to bottom.

21. Tie a 6-Strand Diamond Knot (see Page 58) with the horizontal cords.

22. Carefully snip and singe the cord ends to complete the Secret Compartment Fob.

23. To utilize the secret compartment, split the cord ends apart…

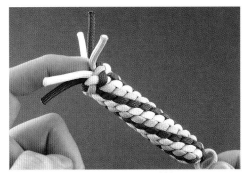

24. …and press the item you'd like to store into the space within.

25. Allow the cord ends to fall back into place to hide the secret compartment opening.

26. To retrieve your item, split the cord ends apart…

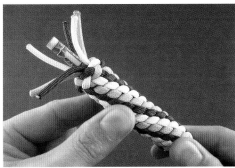

27. …and compress the base of the piece. This will push your item out of the secret compartment, slightly.

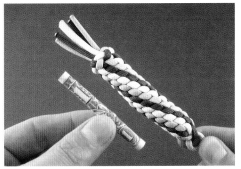

28. From there, simply pull your item out.

HEXAGONAL SECRET COMPARTMENT FOB

Just like the original version, the Hexagonal Secret Compartment Fob can be used to hide items in its hollow elongated center. Only in this case, a switchbacked weaving technique is used to assemble the piece, generating a hexagonal rather than cylindrical shape.

Cord Used: *Three 5 ft. (1.5 m) Cords = 3.5 in. (8.9 cm) Key Fob*

Component Parts: *6-Strand Crown Sinnet + Circular Switchbacked Weave*

1. At the middle of the first cord, make a counterclockwise loop.

2. Lace the second cord through the loop, until its middle is reached.

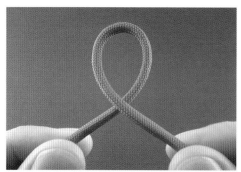

3. Flip the piece over, vertically, slide your forefinger into the loop, and extend the second cord laterally.

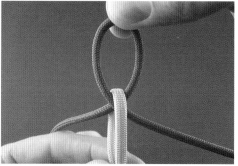

4. Arch the second cord ends over the first, in opposite directions, right cord above left.

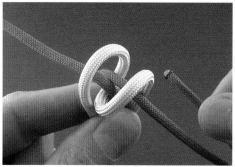

5. Weave the lower cord end over the arch above it…

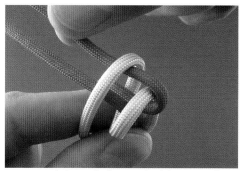

6. …and through the crook of the second arch.

7. Weave the upper cord end over the arch below it…

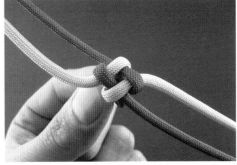

8. …and through the crook of the second arch, making a Crown Knot.

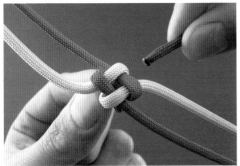

9. Take the tip of the third cord in hand…

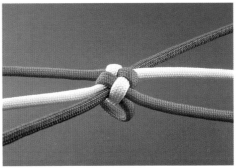

10. …and insert it through the side of the Crown Knot. Tighten the knot firmly around the third cord.

11. Moving clockwise, cross the top cord over the upper right cord below it.

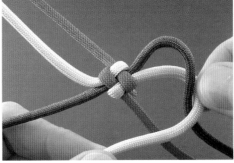

12. Cross the upper right cord over the lower right cord below it.

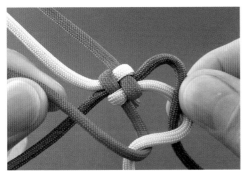

13. Cross the lower right cord over the bottom cord.

14. Cross the bottom cord over the lower left cord above it.

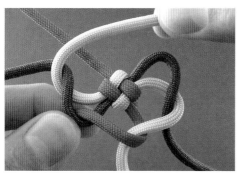

15. Cross the lower left cord over the upper left cord above it.

16. Then insert the upper left cord end over and through the top crook.

17. Adjust the cords until the knot is firm.

18. Moving counterclockwise, cross the lower right cord over the upper right cord above it.

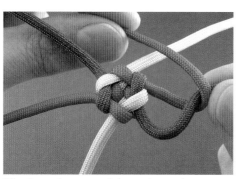

19. Cross the upper right cord over the top cord.

20. Cross the top cord over the upper left cord below it.

21. Cross the upper left cord over the lower left cord below it.

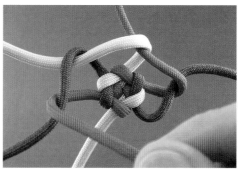

22. Cross the lower left cord over the bottom cord.

23. Then insert the bottom cord end over and through the lower right crook.

24. Adjust the cords until the knot is firm.

25. Repeat Steps 11 through 24 until a minimum 5 in. (12.7 cm) of cord ends remain.

26. **Note:** The center of the Secret Compartment Fob should be open and hollow.

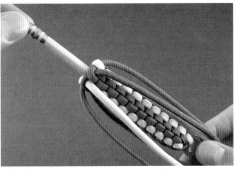

27. If it is not, use a pencil to widen the center, top to bottom.

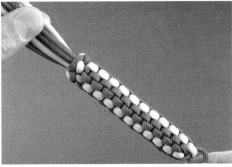

28. Tie a 6-Strand Diamond Knot (see Page 58) with the horizontal cords.

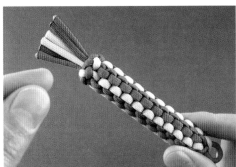

29. Carefully snip and singe the cord ends to complete the Hexagonal Secret Compartment Fob.

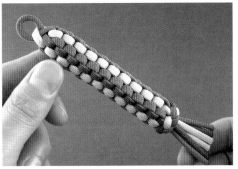

30. For instructions on how to utilize your secret compartment fob, see Page 129.

BOLT BASKET

The Bolt Basket illustrates another innovative application of locking Slip Knots. Tied in series from a Crown Knot base, the locking Slip Knots form a sturdy yet flexible basket that holds mini-crossbow bolts (thus the tie's name) for storage or tossing to another person.

Cord Used: *Four 6 ft. (1.8 m) Cords = 4.5 in. (11.4 cm) Long by 1.5 in. (3.8 cm) Wide Basket*

Component Parts: *Double-Corded Crown Knot + Locking Slip Knots + Square Knots*

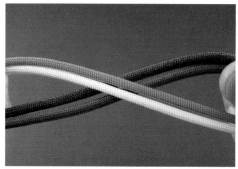

1. Separate the cords into two sets of two. Then cross the sets over each other at their middles, making an **X**.

2. Arch the bottom set of cord ends over the top, in opposite directions, right cords above left.

3. Weave the lower cord ends over the double arches above them…

4. …and through the crooks of the second double arches.

5. Weave the upper cord ends over the double arches below them…

6. …and through the crooks of the second double arches. Tighten the Crown Knot made, firmly.

7. Flip the Crown Knot over, horizontally.

8. Make a counterclockwise loop with the top right cord.

9. Bight the top right cord's running end through the loop…

10. …and tighten, leaving a 0.5 in. (1.3 cm) loop in the Slip Knot made.

11. Moving counterclockwise, insert the cord to the left through the loop of the Slip Knot.

12. Then tighten the Slip Knot firmly around the cord.

13. Continue forward repeating Steps 8 through 12…

14. …making a Slip Knot…

15. …with each cord…

16. …that tightens firmly…

17. …around the cord to its left…

18. …until…

19. …one complete counterclockwise rotation is made.

20. Then continue forward repeating Steps 8 through 12, shaping away from the Crown Knot…

21. …until a minimum 5 in. (12.7 cm) of cord ends remain.

22. Note: The center of the Bolt Basket should be open and hollow.

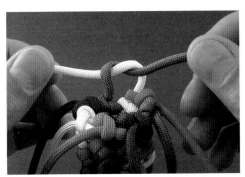

23. Between the last cord looped by a Slip Knot and the cord left of it, tie an Overhand Knot, left cord over right.

24. Tighten the Overhand Knot firmly.

25. Tie a second Overhand Knot, atop the first, right cord over left.

26. Tighten the second Overhand Knot firmly against the one below, making a Square Knot.

27. Between the left cord of the Square Knot and the cord left of it, tie an Overhand Knot, left cord over right.

28. Tighten the Overhand Knot firmly.

29. Tie a second Overhand Knot, atop the first, right cord over left.

30. Tighten the second Overhand Knot firmly against the one below, making a Square Knot.

31. Repeat Steps 27 through 30 six more times.

32. Carefully snip and singe the knot ends.

33. Take the bottom and top of the Bolt Basket in hand and twist its (hollow) center open.

34. The completed Bolt Basket filled with aluminum mini-crossbow bolts.

UTILITY KNIFE POUCH

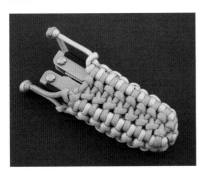

The Utility Knife Pouch takes the Backbone Bar tying technique (see PFT-V1) to the next level. Used to generate a utility knife-sized pouch fitted with loops for a belt, this technique can also be used to make a sheath for a fixed knife blade—just increase the lengths of the cords used.

Cord Used: *Two 12 ft. (3.7 m) Cords = 3.5 in. (8.9 cm) Long by 2 in. (5.1 cm) Wide Pouch*

Component Parts: *Crown Knot + Slip Knot Loops + Backbone Bar + Overhand Knots*

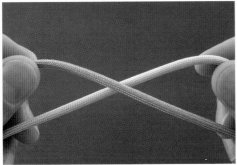

1. Cross the first cord over the second at their middles, making an **X**.

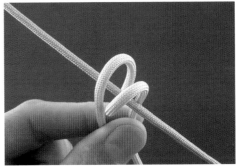

2. Arch the second cord ends over the first, in opposite directions, right cord above left.

3. Weave the lower cord end over the arch above it…

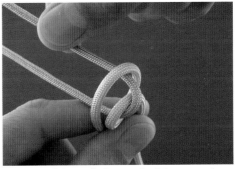

4. …and through the crook of the second arch.

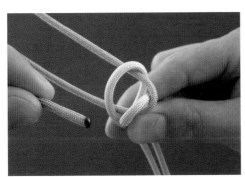

5. Weave the upper cord end over the arch below it…

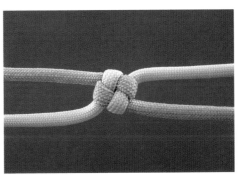

6. …and through the crook of the second arch. Tighten the Crown Knot made, firmly.

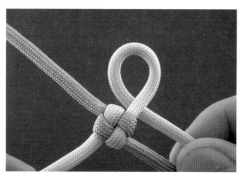

7. Make a clockwise loop with the upper right cord.

8. Bight the upper right cord's running end through the loop…

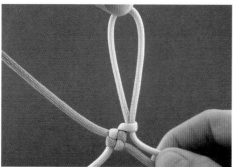

9. …and tighten, leaving a 3.5 in. (8.9 cm) long loop in the Slip Knot made.

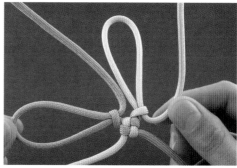

10. Moving counterclockwise, repeat Steps 7 through 9…

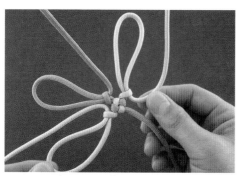

11. …until every cord…

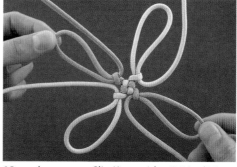

12. …becomes a Slip Knot with a 3.5 in. (8.9 cm) loop in it.

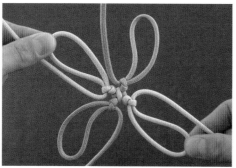

13. Flip the piece over, horizontally.

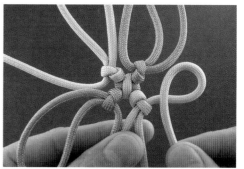

14. Make a counterclockwise loop with the lower right cord.

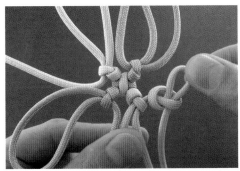

15. Bight the lower right cord's running end through the loop…

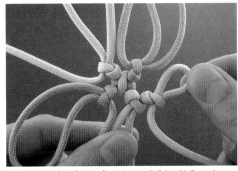

16. …and tighten, leaving a 0.5 in. (1.3 cm) loop in the Slip Knot made.

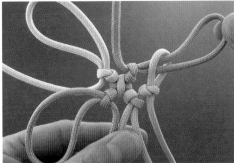

17. Insert the long loop to the left, through the loop of the short Slip Knot.

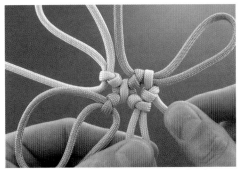

18. Then tighten the short Slip Knot firmly around the long loop.

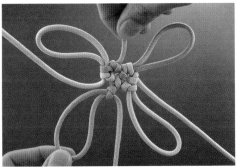

19. Moving counterclockwise, repeat Steps 14 through 18…

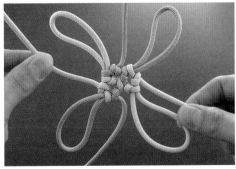

20. …until every cord…

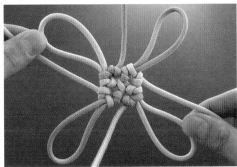

21. …becomes a Slip Knot that tightens firmly around the loop to its left.

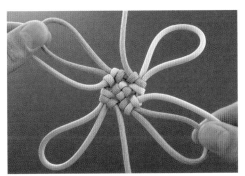

22. Flip the piece over, horizontally.

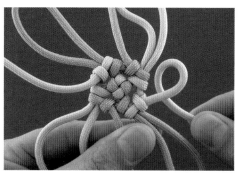

23. Make a clockwise loop with the lower right cord.

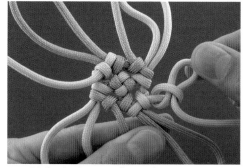

24. Bight the lower right cord's running end through the loop…

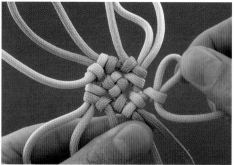

25. …and tighten, leaving a 0.5 in. (1.3 cm) loop in the Slip Knot made.

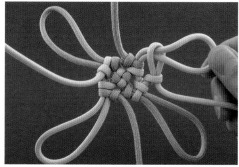

26. Insert the long loop to the left through the loop of the short Slip Knot.

27. Then tighten the short Slip Knot firmly around the long loop.

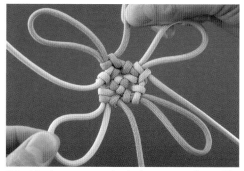

28. Moving counterclockwise, repeat Steps 23 through 27…

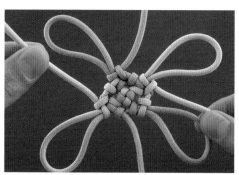

29. …until every cord…

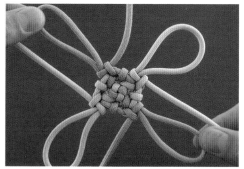

30. …becomes a Slip Knot that tightens firmly around the loop to its left.

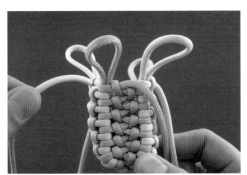

31. Repeat Steps 13 through 30, shaping the pouch away from the top of the Crown Knot…

32. …until the loops at the top of the pouch are 0.5 in. (1.3 cm) long.

33. To lock the piece in place, take a cord end…

34. …and insert it through its nearest loop.

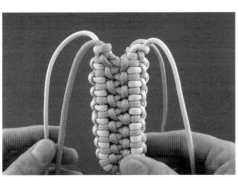

35. Repeat Steps 33 and 34 with all remaining cord ends.

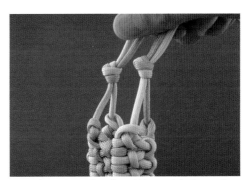

36. Then tie an Overhand Knot with the ends of the front and back cord ends.

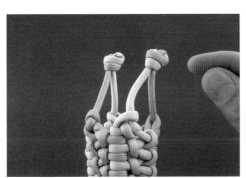

37. Carefully snip and singe the Overhand Knot ends.

38. The completed Utility Knife Pouch looped through a belt.

DRAGON EGG POUCH

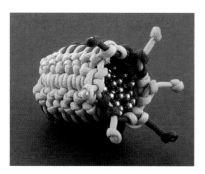

The Dragon Egg Pouch is the 6-strand "inside-out" version of the Utility Knife Pouch. Providing a wider storage area and an easy-to-open, easy-to-close top, the piece makes a great slingshot ammo bag, as shown in the completed project image to the left.

Cord Used: *Three 12 ft. (3.7 m) Cords = 4.0 in. (10.2 cm) Long by 2.5 in. (6.4 cm) Wide Pouch*

Component Parts: *6-Strand Crown Knot + Slip Knot Loops + Backbone Bar + Cow Hitches + Overhand Knots*

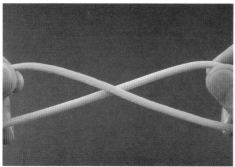

1. Cross the first cord over the second at their middles, making an **X**.

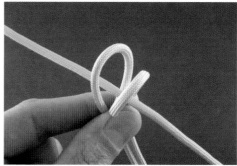

2. Arch the second cord ends over the first, in opposite directions, right cord above left.

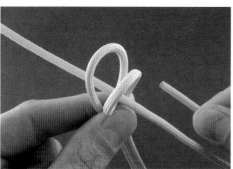

3. Weave the lower cord end over the arch above it…

4. …and through the crook of the second arch.

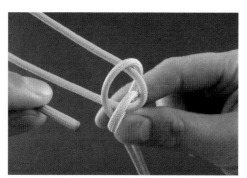

5. Weave the upper cord end over the arch below it…

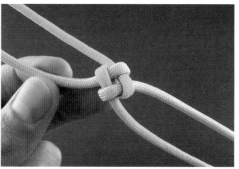

6. …and through the crook of the second arch, making a Crown Knot.

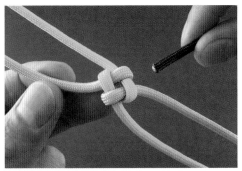

7. Take the tip of the third cord in hand…

8. …and insert it through the side of the Crown Knot. Tighten the knot firmly around the third cord.

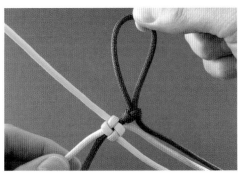

9. Make a counterclockwise loop with the upper right cord.

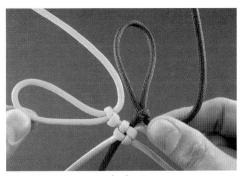

10. Bight the upper right cord's running end through the loop…

11. …and tighten, leaving a 4 in. (10.2 cm) long loop in the Slip Knot made.

12. Moving counterclockwise…

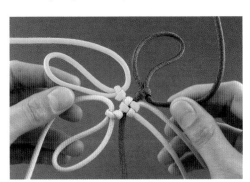

13. …repeat Steps 9 through 11…

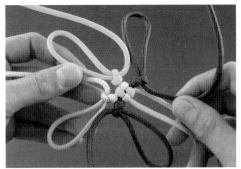

14. …until every cord…

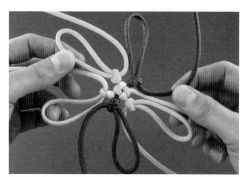

15. …becomes a Slip Knot…

16. …with a 4 in. (10.2 cm) loop in it.

17. Flip the piece over, horizontally.

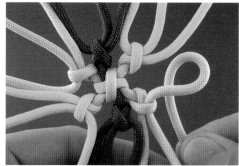

18. Make a clockwise loop with the middle right cord.

19. Bight the middle right cord's running end through the loop…

20. …and tighten, leaving a 0.5 in. (1.3 cm) loop in the Slip Knot made.

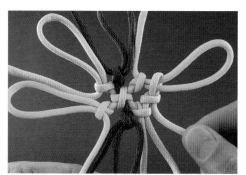

21. Insert the long loop, to the left, through the loop of the short Slip Knot.

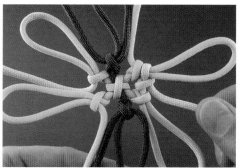

22. Then tighten the short Slip Knot firmly around the long loop.

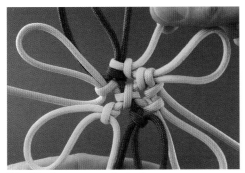

23. Moving counterclockwise…

24. …repeat Steps 18 through 22…

25. …until every cord…

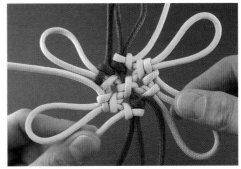

26. …becomes a Slip Knot…

27. …that tightens firmly around the loop to its left.

28. Flip the piece over, horizontally.

29. Make a counterclockwise loop with the middle right cord.

30. Bight the middle right cord's running end through the loop…

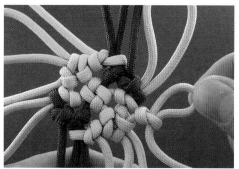

31. …and tighten, leaving a 0.5 in. (1.3 cm) loop in the Slip Knot made.

32. Insert the long loop, to the left, through the loop of the short Slip Knot.

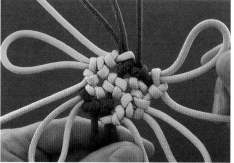

33. Then tighten the short Slip Knot firmly around the long loop.

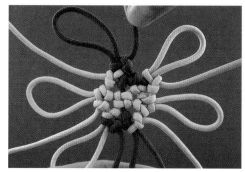

34. Moving counterclockwise…

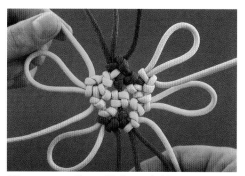

35. …repeat Steps 29 through 33…

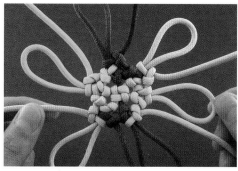

36. …until every cord…

37. …becomes a Slip Knot…

38. …that tightens firmly around the loop to its left.

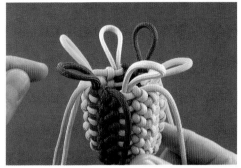

39. Repeat Steps 17 through 38, shaping the pouch away from the top of the Crown Knot…

40. …until the loops at the top of the pouch are 1.5 in. (3.8 cm) long.

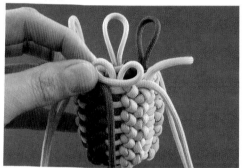

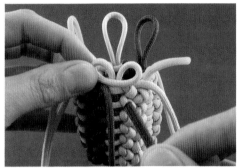

41. To lock the piece in place, bend a loop down over itself, making two loops from one.

42. Then take the cord end left of the loops in hand…

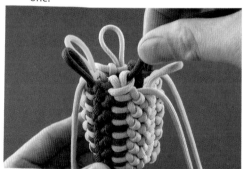

43. …and insert it through the front of the left loop and back of the right loop, making a Cow Hitch around a cord.

44. Repeat Steps 41 through 43 with all remaining loops and cord ends.

45 Stretch the pouch open as wide as you can.

46. Then take a cord and make a counter-clockwise loop at its base.

47. Insert the cord's running end through the loop, making a single-cord Overhand Knot.

48. Repeat Steps 46 and 47 with all remaining cords.

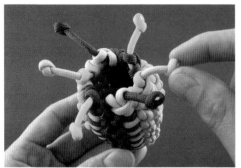

49. Make a single cord Overhand Knot at the tip of all cords. Then carefully snip and singe the knot ends.

50. The completed Dragon Egg Pouch.

623.8882 LENZEN V.2
Lenzen, J.D.,
Paracord fusion ties.
R2001252606 PALMETTO

ODC